Small Business Turnaround Plan

Your Complete Guide to Getting Back to Profitability While Saving Your Sanity

Byron Walker

CONTENTS

ACKNOWLEDGMENTS

Writing a book is hard. Turning around a company is even harder. I'd like to acknowledge those who helped me get through my own business turnaround.

For those friends who took the time to meet with me and hear me out, thank you. At last count, there were 45 amazing friends that met with me to discuss my situation. You listened to my fears, the uncertainty and, at times, my shear panic. I could see the look of concern as you consoled me, yet conveying that everything was going to be okay. Thank you Zack DeLisa for teaching me the path to financial savviness. Matt Smith, thanks for telling me the things I didn't want to hear. James Webb, now I can say, "you were right," regarding layoffs coming in three waves. And a big thanks to Scott Palat for the one big idea that helped me connect the dots with my turnaround.

Without my EO (Entrepreneurs Organization) forum, I'm not sure how I could have gotten through the turnaround. As we met each month, and the updates I provided continued to get worse, your confidence in me never wavered. You provided incredible insights, valuable experience shares and helped in finding my blind spots. And thank you Kelli Sexton for suggesting I document my turnaround journey so I could eventually get this book written.

My family is the greatest area of gratitude and the one thing that will always pull me through tough times. My amazing wife, Maribel, was not just supportive and loving during these tough times, she encouraged me to keep fighting and held the confidence that the downturn was only temporary.

Finally, I'd like to thank the crew at ProduceMyBook.com. Their combination of process, patience and gentle prodding helped me stay on-track to complete the book in a timely fashion.

INTRODUCTION

Business downturns suck. ~Byron

If you are reading these words, then odds are your business needs help. Likely, your entire life has been turned upside down with an unbearable amount of stress and anxiety.

When your business is suffering, you are suffering. Entrepreneurs are deeply connected to their companies, and when one is not doing well, the other feels it.

The bright side is that there is a way out, and the *Small Business Turnaround Plan* can help you find it. In this book, you will learn proven strategies for turning your small to medium sized business around. You will discover specific action steps you can take to get your business back to profitability in the shortest time possible. If you follow the tools outlined in this book, I am confident that you have an excellent chance of saving your business.

There is a stipulation with this promise, however. **You must act now**. You will need to read this book quickly and take action to start creating your turnaround immediately.

Every week you delay creating a turnaround plan is another week you fall deeper into trouble. When a business is losing money, you can almost hear the clock's tick-tock sound. Time is money, and in this case, the losses add up with each passing day, week, and month that you fail to act.

Unless you have a bottomless cashflow source or investors willing to throw money at the problem, you will have limited time to fix your failing business. Every day your company operates at a loss it digs the grave just a little deeper. Eventually, you will find yourself out of cash and out of business.

Time is critical. Do not wait another day. Dive into this book, take notes, and start creating your turnaround plan now. Tick-tock. Tick-tock.

Who Needs the *Small Business Turnaround Plan*?

This book was written for the $1 million+ annual revenue entrepreneur who will do whatever it takes to save his or her business. If you are below $1 million in annual gross revenue, you can still benefit from this book. However, the examples I share will resonate most with those managing a multi-million-dollar company.

Businesses with revenue of $20 million or more will also benefit from this book, although you may need to modify some of the strategies. For example, if a larger company has investors behind it, those investors are often okay with exchanging profits for growth, so wiping out losses is not as urgent an issue. For most companies who cannot afford to lose money on an ongoing basis, this book is precisely what you need.

As this book goes to print, small businesses everywhere are navigating their way through the COVID-19 crisis. Government stimulus plans helped cover some of the short-term losses, but it was only a Band-Aid.

What struggling businesses need is something much more meaningful and enduring. If your business finds itself in the middle of a downturn, what it needs is a quickly executed turnaround plan.

The reasons behind your downturn could be numerous, from COVID-19 to an economic downturn or market shifts. Maybe you lost a significant client, or your competition is moving in and grabbing market share. The nature of the downturn varies from one business to another, but they all have similar characteristics. Declining revenue and mounting expenses blend to create a toxic combination that will send the best of companies into a tailspin that is backbreaking to reverse.

For most small businesses on a tight budget, hiring a professional turnaround expert, also known as a chief restructuring officer, is just not possible. Turnaround experts often charge hundreds of thousands of dollars for just a few months of their time. Most small businesses simply can't afford to hire professional help. The Small Business Turnaround Plan is written for the entrepreneur who must fix their company without the help of a cost prohibitive consultant. This do-it-yourself plan will give you the ideas and tools you need to execute your own turnaround plan.

Keeping Your Sanity is Key

If your business is going through a downturn, then no doubt life is pretty rough right now. Experiencing monthly losses can be devastating for the entrepreneur. It is not only the loss of money that hurts, but also your loss of direction and self-worth. The pride and sense of purpose for many business owners are wrapped up in their company, so a downturn is a significant hit to the ego.

Entrepreneurs have a lot riding on their daily decisions. You have payroll to meet and bills to pay. Your employees, some of whom you have known for years and you consider friends, are depending on you. You may have investors to answer to or personal guarantees on loans leveraging your home. Countless people, including your own family, rely on you to make the right decisions.

So, when your business is suffering, it may feel like the world's weight is on your shoulders. The problems feel monumental when your once profitable company is on the verge of collapsing. You are the one everyone is looking at to fix the problems and to create a turnaround plan.

Through this book, I can become your copilot to help navigate you through the downturn. This book will provide specific how-to strategies for getting back to profitability while also helping you maneuver through the emotional journey. Yes, your goal is to get your business back to profitability, but there are steps you can take along the way that will help manage your mental state as well.

Few books (if any) detail the true impact on the entrepreneur's mental state during a business downturn. The *Small Business Turnaround Plan* can provide the support in saving both your business and your sanity.

How do I know so much about the turnaround journey? I recently survived my own business downturn, and it was devastating. Throughout this book, I am open and honest about my own personal crusade to turn my small business around. My hope is by being vulnerable and sharing my struggles, this will help you to face your own difficult situations with confidence and come out the other side better than you were before.

The Six Steps of a Turnaround

The *Small Business Turnaround Plan* is divided into six main sections. They include:

Section 1: Keeping your sanity–Watching your baby (the business you raised from the spark of an idea) suffer and approach the brink of failure is a rough road. You need to stay sharp and focused so that you can mentally endure the upcoming challenge.

Section 2: Mastering your financials–Even if you hate accounting, this book will show you how to master your financials. You will be introduced to a method of monitoring and projecting cashflow and creating a financial turnaround plan that will get you back to profitability in the shortest amount of time possible.

Section 3: Optimizing your revenue–If you take only one insight from this book, let it be this. The secret to reviving your company is not as simple as "increasing sales." In fact, you may discover by reducing poorly performing revenue your recovery could be faster. We will also focus on optimizing your healthy revenue and then finding ways of increasing it.

Section 4: Cutting expenses and finding efficiencies–This part can be tough, but I will show you ways to make it more tolerable. Make no mistake, reducing expenses is the fastest way back to profitability. This, combined with operational efficiencies, can ensure you will stay profitable moving forward.

Section 5: Finding labor efficiencies–Saving your company and returning to profitability may require staff reduction. No, *do not* put this book down yet! I will show you how to make this process as painless as possible for all parties. The goal is to look back with dignity for handling this sensitive (but necessary) responsibility in the right way.

Section 6: Implementing your turnaround plan–
This is where it all comes together into a cohesive plan to save your business. Use the examples and action steps provided to customize your own turnaround plan.

Avoiding Common Turnaround Pitfalls

There are several common pitfalls when it comes to turning around a failing business; the first is relating to revenue. As mentioned before, the secret to reviving your company is not as simple as merely increasing revenue. As I steered through my own company's downturn, I got plenty of bad advice, including the misconception that revenue will solve all problems. "Just sell more," was the advice a highly paid consultant provided. I will share more of this story in Section 3 and explain why that was horrible advice. The ultimate solution to fixing my company turned out to be the complete opposite.

Another area of danger is reducing expenses and laying off employees without a plan. Yes, there will be expenses cut, and most likely you will have to trim down your team, but broad advice such as "cut all expenses or staff by 50%" can create more problems than solutions. By taking a more strategic approach, you will find ways to do more with less and increase your labor efficiency.

The last area of concern relates to your financial statements. Some entrepreneurs think they can rely on their accountants or bookkeepers to do all the heavy lifting when it comes to financial reports. The truth is it will be essential that you personally dive into your historic books and lead the efforts in creating financial forecasts. But don't worry, I will explain how to read and analyze your financial statements in a simple and straightforward manner.

Lessons From the Survival Frog Turnaround

My business is in the *survival* industry. Ironic, I know. SurvivalFrog.com sells survival and outdoor gear direct to consumers online. Topline revenue before our downturn was around $9 million, and I was making a nice profit. With 27 employees, an office, and a warehouse for product fulfillment, there were many moving parts.

Survival Frog was growing, and we were focused on the typical challenges of hiring good people, managing data, and the never-ending list of essential projects. I enjoyed running the business and was excited for the future.

I had delegated most of the day-to-day activities off my plate, so I primarily focused on managing my team and the growth of the business. Our company culture was solid, we had a great operating system, and our management team was strong. We made the INC 5000 list and were in the media a few times a year. Business was good. Life was good. Until it wasn't.

Our first month of losses happened in December of 2017, but I did not realize what had happened until late February of 2018. At the time, my accounting department closed the financial books so slowly that I often did not know how much profit we made for a few months. When those profits became losses, the delayed reporting got scary.

The day is sketched onto my brain in permanent ink...finding out that we had suffered losses during December, which is typically our best sales month of the year. Then learning we also had massive losses in January. The numbers looked even worse for February, and we were heading into our slow time of the year. Oh, boy.

The entire survival market was in freefall and Survival Frog, one of the largest companies in its niche, was out in front crashing nose-first into the sand. The downturn was caused primarily by a shift in political power in the United States, with demand for survival products plummeting soon after President Trump took office.

The losses were staggering and the problems plentiful. Everywhere I looked, something within the business was breaking. With each passing month, things just seemed to get worse. It was a complete shit-show. I felt as if I was hurtling 200 MPH towards a cliff of doom and was struggling to find the steering wheel.

This was the hardest thing I have ever been through, and I struggled emotionally. One of my friends summed it up well when he said a major downturn is "like watching a child die." I watched the company I started over ten years ago get to the brink of disaster, and I felt there was nothing I could do about it.

We had gone from a thriving, growing business to a failing company on the verge of bankruptcy. It was a humbling experience, full of extreme challenges and never-ending drama. For the first several months I was paralyzed by fear and not sure of my next steps.

Over time, my team and I started to figure things out. We got control over the financials and started to forecast cashflow. Then came the gut-wrenching task of cutting costs and letting staff go. Over the course of several layoffs, my once-bustling office with 27 employees eventually shrank to just five employees who worked virtually. We restructured almost every department and implemented efficiencies so we could operate with less.

More details of the Survival Frog turnaround story can be found throughout the book, but in short, we did a significant overhaul of the entire company. What remained is an amazingly efficient and profitable company, which is a joy to operate.

Moving Your Mind Beyond Impossible

For each step along the way, there were monumental problems to solve and plenty of self-doubts. I wish I had this book to guide me through the process and give me the confidence that I could overcome the seemingly impossible scenarios I faced. For most of those tough situations, however, my initial response was simply, "That's impossible."

Cutting revenue on purpose? Laying off employees I had known for years? Restructuring departments that I knew nothing about? Preparing financial forecasts? It all seemed impossible to me at the time.

As you work through the different ideas and recommendations in this book, I ask one crucial thing. When you arrive at an "impossible" situation or need to make an unbearable decision, I ask that you push through it as if it *is* possible. Allow your mind to move beyond impossible and find a way. Many things seem impossible when we first encounter them, but after further investigation, there is almost always a way to make it a reality.

Survival Frog had to make many "impossible" situations become a reality in order to survive. When we were done with our business turnaround, and the red numbers finally turned black, the company had seen a drop from $9 million in annual revenue to $3 million. But here is the kicker…we were just as profitable as before the downturn. Yes, that's right! The profit we earned at $3 million revenue was the *same dollar amount* as when we were at $9 million. We tripled the net profit percentage!

Survival Frog's turnaround took well over a year. It was not easy, but when complete, it produced a highly profitable and streamlined company. It is now more enjoyable to run the business and requires less of my time. The business is much more predictable, and I get actionable data from my financial reporting each month.

I want you to have the same positive results with your business turnaround. By moving your mind beyond what appears to be impossible, you can take a business that appears doomed and transform it into a better version of the company you once had.

If you cannot see the way forward and do not know the next steps, you are not alone. I was there. I was confused. I was desperate. The good news is that once you start crafting your turnaround plan, everything starts to come into focus. Once you successfully implement the turnaround plan, you will be pleasantly surprised by what you will find on the other side.

Finding Your Turnaround Gift

Successfully executing a turnaround plan produces a fantastic surprise gift at the end. The gift is that your company is a far better company than it was before. The gift is how much you learn throughout the experience. The gift is your personal growth and the wisdom you obtain.

I don't expect you to read these words and be excited and happy about the trip ahead. The journey still sucks. The glass is still half-empty (actually, it's broken and spilling water all over the place). But I ask that you have faith that all will turn out okay in the end. **Something good will come from this.** It is hard to see now, but eventually this adversity will make you a better and stronger person. If you are actively looking for the gift within the challenge at hand, you will find it.

One of the quotes that got me through my own turnaround is this:

"Bad things don't happen to me. Bad things happen for me. For me to be better, be smarter, and for me to grow."

History has shown that businesses facing challenging times create amazing innovations and the results often create far better companies in the end. This is your chance to see your business run more efficiently, with your profit margins higher than you could have imagined.

Today I invite you to commit to turn your business around. Step up to the challenge and make those difficult decisions ahead of you with confidence. I encourage you to develop a turnaround plan that will get you back to profitability, not just for the money, but because you deserve to have a healthy and profitable business. You deserve to feel successful and proud of what you have built.

I may not know you, but I do know you have had to fight to get your business started. You have gone through challenging times in the past. I am confident you have the strength to get through this latest challenge. You've got this!

Taking Action Now

The fact is that most failing businesses could be saved with an effective turnaround plan. However, only a small percentage of those businesses will survive. Ironically, the leading indicator of whether a company will survive is far less about the turnaround plan itself. Instead, the primary indicator of success is how fast the owner or CEO responds to the downturn and starts making changes.

Let me say it a different way. **The success of your business is dependent on how fast you respond and take action towards your turnaround.**

Time is not your friend. When you run out of cash, you run out of time. The sooner you start cutting costs and making bold decisions on the turnaround, the better your odds of survival.

Never in history has a small business owner ever "overreacted" by cutting expenses or making massive changes too quickly. It does not work that way. Instead, business owners find themselves in an endless loop of agonizing delays, plagued by insecurity and fear of change.

For many entrepreneurs, there is a strong desire to protect their employees. Owners try not to "rock the boat" and instead attempt to provide the illusion of a secure and stable company. Push back when you find yourself trying to minimize the severity of the problem or delaying decisions that could scare your team.

Big bold decisions that are executed quickly are needed during a business turnaround. You must rock the boat.

Taking decisive action early in the process gives you a critical advantage. Remember, time is not on your side. You must create your turnaround plan and execute it immediately.

Creating Your Own Turnaround Plan

So, what exactly is a turnaround plan? First, it is a "plan," not something you make up along the way. It is an actionable strategy that you document in writing.

By creating forecasted profit and loss statements (P&Ls) and playing out different turnaround scenarios, you can test the viability of each idea. Before you make any big changes, you will know what the most likely outcome of those actions would be. The turnaround plan will clarify which projects need to be put on hold, and which you should move forward on with guns a-blazing.

The turnaround plan is also something that evolves over time. It is not a rigid plan but rather something in a constant state of flux. The turnaround plan is never "perfect." Waiting to get started until you have everything 100% ready is the kiss of death. You need to start now and then make course corrections as your business continues to change. Your business *will* change; expect it.

Having a plan in writing will give you the needed clarity to rally your employees and reduce anxiety levels related to the turnaround. The turnaround plan gives you something to move towards which helps everyone get behind the upcoming changes that are needed.

No two turnaround plans are the same. Your turnaround plan will be unique and different from any other business. This book explains the fundamental strategies that helped my business as well as other businesses I have helped along the way. I packed this book full of best practices and ideas that will help you craft your own unique turnaround strategy.

Every week you delay is just another layer that you will need to unbury your company from. Time is of the essence. Now jump in and start your own turnaround success story. Tick-tock; tick-tock.

SECTION ONE
KEEPING YOUR SANITY

Bad things don't happen to me. Bad things happen for me. For me to learn, for me to grow and for me to be a better person. ~Byron

You are in the middle of a nightmare.

"Company downturn," while an accurate description, does not do justice to the chaos happening all around you. Twenty-four hours a day, seven days a week, you are being barraged by negativity and problems. Even on a good day, you find yourself trying desperately just to hang on. You have no choice but to figure out how (or even if) you can fix your company.

My downturn was the hardest business challenge I have ever endured. It was earth-shattering. Some days, it seemed like everybody and everything was out to get me.

Survival Frog is much more than just a company to me–it is like a child I have raised. I suspect you feel the same about your company. You created it from nothing; it is your life, your passion, your WHY. It feels like the core of who you are. Now that it is falling apart, it feels like you are losing your baby. It is devastating.

Well-meaning allies will assure you that your business does not define you and that you can be a success even as your business is failing. Let me be honest with you; those comments are not much help when your business and personal life are tipped upside down.

You will question your sanity many times throughout the turnaround journey. I believe everything happens for a reason, and during these challenges, you will learn a lot about yourself.

Bad things do not happen to you. Bad things happen for you so that you learn, grow—and eventually have a better business.

It is up to you to turn this thing around. There is no one better suited to succeed at this than you. It is up to you to keep your sanity despite all the madness around you.

Step one to turning your business around is to learn how to stay sane throughout the downturn. The assault on your business and livelihood is nothing more than a new challenge, and when you meet that challenge head-on, amazing things can happen.

You have overcome some enormous challenges in the past. Starting your business was a massive challenge that you managed to get through, and I am sure there were dark days early on. You overcame those tests and you will overcome this one.

However, that is only possible when you learn how to keep your sanity during your business turnaround.

SECTION ONE: KEEPING YOUR SANITY

CHAPTER 1
PREPARE FOR THINGS
TO GET WORSE

Trouble never comes alone. ~Russian Proverb

When it rains, it pours. In a business downturn, it storms...deluges...monsoons...floods. In a downturn, there is only one thing you can expect. Things will get worse before they get better.

You will have numerous issues that you will not see coming. Some days you will feel like things cannot possibly get worse. Then they will get worse.

"Wow, thanks, Byron, great pep talk. I can't wait to get started on my own turnaround."

I get it. During Survival Frog's downturn, the garbage just piled on. We were threatened with lawsuits. We got scammed. We got stuck with excess inventory. We were audited. Our bank threatened to call our bank loans. To add insult to injury, as my business hemorrhaged $50,000+ losses per month, my refrigerator at home died. So did the dishwasher. The exterior painting project I had been putting off at my house became an urgent requirement. Not one, but both of my cars broke down, and I had to replace them. I just could not get a break.

It was maddening to deal with everything that went wrong. It got so bad that I would just laugh (read: whimper) when another fiasco happened.

I relied heavily on the support of my business friends during the downturn. It helped me to tell them about my latest trials and tribulations as I fought to save my company. They often admired me for being so calm. I did not have the heart to tell them my "calm" was just shock, like a deer in the headlights of an oncoming semi-truck.

As someone who has experienced what you are going through today, I can assure you that eventually the onslaught of challenges will subside. Someday, the things that can break or go wrong run their course.

Life will kick you when you are down, and there will be days when life kicks a few extra times, just to be sure you feel it. Sooner or later, you will run out of bad stuff that can happen. A few good things will happen, and the tide will begin to turn. It will take time to work everything out, but almost all problems have a solution.

I want to share several isolated problems that I experienced during the downturn and turnaround of Survival Frog. The "fast forward" result confirms the theory that all the bad stuff will work out.

Nearly every crisis resulted in a resolution that helped Survival Frog, and me, become more resilient, efficient, and profitable than we were before the downturn. While your challenges may be different from mine, these examples show how most bad things turn out okay with time.

Pressure from the bank–Our bank threatened to call our line of credit due, and because we had missed a covenant deadline in our loan agreement, they threatened to "restructure" a half-million-dollar term loan.

Fast forward 12 months–After several uncomfortable conversations with the bank, we managed to convince them we had a good turnaround strategy and were able to keep all loans in place.

Legal issues–An ex-employee planted pirated software on one of Survival Frog's computers, and then reported us to the software police (yes, they do exist!) in exchange for a "whistleblower fee." We had never even used the software, and yet the fine was $35,000. You cannot make this stuff up!

Fast forward two months–I was able to negotiate the fine down to $8,000, which they accepted over four monthly payments.

Threats of lawsuits–When an email service provider was unable to perform the services they agreed to, I was confident that they would void the two-year contract. Instead, their lawyers demanded we pay them the entire $165,000 contract price, despite being unable to use their services.

Fast forward six months–We negotiated the price down to $12,000 (plus $5,000 in legal fees). Ironically, that is the amount we owed them for the time we used their services.

Government audits–It just would not be a party without the government getting involved. The State of Colorado found that some of our contractors should have been employees and demanded we pay additional taxes. In addition, the IRS had issues with some previous tax returns and levied fines against Survival Frog. We had never had issues with any type of audits for the first nine years in business, so naturally, this would happen during our downturn.

Fast forward–The IRS waived all fees, and the Colorado taxes were just a few hundred dollars. So much worry and stress over nothing.

Product defect issues–We had somehow made it nine years without any major product defect issues. When we were at our lowest, however, we had plenty of them, including damage to property.

Fast forward–Of course, we had to pay for the damage, but thankfully our customer was happy.

Cease & desist letters–When our top product looked like it could save the day with all the revenue it was generating, we received a letter from the patent holder (unknown to us until then) and had to stop selling the product.

Fast forward–We were able to liquidate the inventory and use the cash to fund operating costs. A few months later the demand for that product declined and our competition found themselves with extra stock they could not sell. We got off lucky.

Unpaid bills–Several vendors suddenly billed us for past-due invoices we had not seen before. Worse yet, once we investigated it, they were right! We were on the hook for payments of $5,000 and $15,000 that we had not planned. Oops! We also found customers that we forgot to invoice that owed us money, although they were not so fast to pay us what was due.

Fast forward a few months–The amount we owed to vendors was almost the same amount owed to us. So that problem balanced itself out.

Lingering skeletons–Once we began to let employees go, we found several examples of misuse of company money. We were paying for old web servers we had stopped using years ago but no one bothered to discontinue. We found that employees had purchased items for personal use with company funds. My favorite was when we found "company loans" that I never knew about.

Fast forward–Although it was disrespectful to the company and to me personally, I also learned that I needed to put more systems in place to avoid this happening again. I am a better manager now because of these challenges.

Even the wins come wrapped in issues–We decided to close the office and find a tenant to sublet the remaining three years of the five-year office/warehouse lease. We found a great sub-tenant that was willing to pay more than our current rent amount. It was a great "win," except that our landlord would not approve the new tenant unless we shared the extra rental profit. Sometimes, even the "wins" come wrapped up in some issues you must pull apart.

Fast forward–After a few difficult conversations (with lawyers involved), the landlord finally approved the sublease, and I profited each month on the deal. Go, team!

Why am I sharing this laundry list of unfortunate events my company went through during our downturn? To show that things usually turn out okay. Make no mistake, for each issue that came up (and there were many challenges that I did not list here), it was devastating and felt like a huge setback. It felt like death by a thousand needles (big thick needles), but each challenge taught us something new.

While it did not seem like it at the time, looking back, it feels like it was just a part of the process. You get kicked when you are down, but it sure toughens you up.

Chapter 1: Action Steps

Consider the following:

- ➤ What is your list of "bad luck" events that have happened to you up to this point?
- ➤ How could these prove to be a good thing in the future?
- ➤ You will need to push yourself on this exercise because it is challenging to see future beneficial outcomes in the midst of chaos.

SECTION ONE: KEEPING YOUR SANITY

CHAPTER 2
AVOIDING THE VICTIM MINDSET

*I can't change the direction of the wind but I can adjust my sails to always reach my destination.
~Jimmy Dean*

Every company's story is different, and I do not know what caused your downturn to start. It may have absolutely nothing to do with you or anyone on your team's actions. Recession, COVID-19, your own market downturn, or another outside force could be the culprit. And that stinks.

This might be a tough pill to swallow, but it does not matter what caused the downturn. You are in a bad situation that will require you to take full responsibility and come up with solutions. There is not enough time for you to feel sorry for yourself, to be the victim, or to participate in a pity party. It does not matter if it's not your fault. Deal with it and move forward.

That might sound harsh but take it from someone who has been there. If you spend your days focused on why you are the victim, you will find plenty of examples to prove your point. Being a victim does absolutely nothing to solve your issue. If instead, you play the part of the brave hero, life will help you become a champion. You are the hero in this story.

Instead of feeling sorry for yourself, take full responsibility and be honest with yourself to get through these challenging times.

Be Brutally Honest

At all costs, do not be in denial of your situation. Burying your head in the sand and ignoring your problems will not help. Some people confuse "staying positive" with denial. They are not the same thing. Honesty means recognizing how dire your situation is, acknowledging that it stinks, and then working on a solution.

Telling yourself that everything will be fine if you only get that one big client, or you increase sales, could be setting yourself up for failure. There is rarely a quick fix and often there are several areas of the business that need your attention.

You may justify that there is no need to cut expenses or lay off employees because once that client is signed, your problems will go away.

What happens if you do not get that big client? What if you do, but things do not just automatically turn themselves around? Denial is dangerous. It delays your timeline in fixing your company, and time is critically important because you are going to run out of cash soon.

Be brutally honest, because lying to yourself is not going to get you anywhere. Acknowledge the reality of the market you are operating in, the state of your company, and your employees. There may be complications with any or all of these, or it may be something completely different. Whatever it is, there is a solution to the issue if you face it head-on and get to work.

Part of being brutally honest is to become very intimate with your financial books. I will walk you through how to dive into your financials in detail in Section 2. As you take a closer look into your financials, I guarantee you will find your company is not as efficient as it should be. Do not dwell on the mistakes. Admit things need to be fixed and get on with it. Prepare yourself to make tough decisions around cost-cutting, labor management, and revenue streams.

Accepting 100% Responsibility

There are countless reasons for a company to go into a tailspin. Maybe you took your eye off the ball or made a few missteps along the way. Perhaps it was COVID-19 or another natural or economic disaster, competitor problems, lawsuits, supply chain issues, government regulations, and more. Maybe, it was just bad luck.

In the case of Survival Frog, there was a significant market shift, and survival gear sales fell 70%. Nearly half of my competitors went out of business, and everyone else was struggling. It would have been easy to blame the market drop for our downturn. For a little bit, I allowed myself to grumble about our nasty luck. After I got over my pity party, I realized that I should have predicted the market shift and taken steps years before to limit the impact. I should have seen it coming. I was responsible for our downturn, not bad luck.

Regardless of what got you to this place, I urge you to take 100% responsibility for your mess. If it rained on your parade, you should have figured out how to alter the weather patterns. If a competitor has come into your space, you should have predicted this and acted years ago. If the market shifted, you should have diversified into additional revenue sources previously. If a global pandemic has shut down your business, then... (you get the idea).

The sobering reality is there were mistakes made in running your company, and most likely, you will find that expenses have gotten away from you.

Even in a market downturn or recession, there are always a few companies that do well. If your company were ultra-efficient and running lean and mean, the recession would hurt a lot less. If you had a healthy balance sheet, you could thrive in market downturns by acquiring assets or buying out your competitors. There is always something more you could have done, so be honest with yourself and then start working toward solutions.

Whatever the reason for your downturn, take 100% responsibility. Then move on.

Chapter 2: Action Steps

Taking into consideration that you are not a victim, contemplate the following. Document your thoughts in writing.

> ➢ Are there challenges within your business that you can take responsibility for? Being brutally honest with your situation and your financials is the first step to a successful turnaround.
> ➢ What are the core reasons for your downturn? This list may grow and change over time.

Take time with this exercise and go deep. Save your notes, and review them later for even greater insights.

SECTION ONE: KEEPING YOUR SANITY

CHAPTER 3
TAKING INVENTORY

It is during our darkest moments that we must focus to see the light. ~Aristotle

When you are fighting the dragon, you often just fixate on that fire-breathing monster in front of you. While you certainly must put out the fires caused by that evil dragon called a downturn, I suggest you dedicate the time to step back and take inventory of your business. Look around and see the entire situation.

SWOT Analysis

Take the time to do a Strength Weakness Opportunity Threats (SWOT) analysis of your business. This is a strategic planning technique. By taking inventory of your company, your team, and yourself, you will see the big picture and find areas that can help you execute your business turnaround.

I recommend you get out of the office to do this, such as a beautiful place in the mountains or on the beach (even a coffee shop will do in a pinch). You can do this later with your team, but do the first round by yourself. When you are relaxed and ready, get a notepad and pencil and begin.

S–Strengths. When you are in a battle, everything looks scary, but you and your company are better than you know. List out all your company's strengths. These may include your team, your industry connections, or your fantastic customer experience. Do not stop until you have listed 20 or 30 strengths, even if some of the points are a little silly.

W–Weaknesses. Now, do the same exercise, but instead of the company's strengths, list all the bad stuff. Where could you be stronger as a company? Go deep here and be brutally honest. Often business owners do not think their baby is ugly, so you may have to push yourself to come up with a good list of 20 or more weaknesses. You do not have to share all these notes with your team.

O–Opportunity. I know the dragon is still breathing down your neck, with its horrible hot steamy breath, but push yourself here and list all the "what if…" scenarios. What areas of the business have you not fully exploited?

What big clients could you land, or what type of marketing could you pursue? Where are other companies seeing success? Are there any pivot ideas you need to explore further? You will not be able to chase all the "potential" opportunities listed here but flushing out all ideas gives you a better perspective of where the smart opportunities are.

T–Threats. Sorry to end on a sour note but list out the various threats to your business. This should not be too hard since several of these issues are currently in full swing. Be sure to add all of "the sky is falling" problems such as product recalls, lawsuits or earthquakes demolishing your office. Include what keeps you up at night. When your business is weak, it is more susceptible to threats such as competition taking your customers. They will try and strike while you are down, so be sure to list all those scenarios.

Once done with your SWOT analysis, put a star next to the top three ideas for each section. These three points are where you can put more energy to shore up your weaknesses and threats and play into your biggest strengths and opportunities.

The point of doing this is to remind you who you are and what is possible, while at the same time acknowledging the downsides you are facing. I hope this helps you step back from the dragon and see the way around it.

Chapter 3: Action Steps

➢ Get out of the office and do your SWOT analysis alone (or with a business partner) - this version of the SWOT is for your eyes only.

➢ Going through the SWOT with your employees is a great exercise to accomplish later.

CHAPTER 4
GETTING OUT OF YOUR HEAD

I don't journal to 'be productive.' I don't do it to find great ideas or to put down prose I can later publish. The pages aren't intended for anyone but me. It's the most cost-effective therapy I've ever found. ~*Tim Ferriss*

The SWOT analysis may have identified several areas that need work in your business. By taking inventory of your strengths and future opportunities, however, you can see that things are not all bad. You now have better clarity on how you got to where you are, and what needs to change in your company.

It would be awesome if that were enough, and merely writing it down would start the wheels turning toward a turnaround.

While clarity is essential, someone must effect change in the company: pull it up out of the muck into a new and improved business. That someone is you. Do not wait another minute. Start your turnaround today!

"Easier said than done, Byron. How the heck do I start?"

I am glad you asked. Throughout the remaining sections of this book, I will share the specific actions you will need to take with your financial statements, operations, and employees so that you can begin your turnaround process immediately.

Take it from someone who has been there: before you can dive into the specifics, you need to act on what is churning around within your head. You need to tame the dragon breathing down your neck (is that a hint of cabbage I smell mixed in with sulfur?).

There are several tactics for keeping your sanity that proved invaluable to me as I worked through Survival Frog's turnaround and will likely be well-used tools in your turnaround toolkit as well. I will explain them in detail here but notice that I have hinted at each one of them already and will continue to encourage their use throughout the rest of the book.

Journaling Your Way to Solutions

You have already started journaling if you took my recommendation and did the Action Steps for each chapter. Documenting the turnaround journey is crucial, but I encourage you to journal your personal life as well. When I read back through my journal and those darkest days, it amazes me. Being able to stand back and witness the chaos and my state of mind during those tough times, gives me a great sense of appreciation and clarity that allows me to see the bigger picture. While it was a rough ride, it gave me incredible insight into myself.

Your journal is more than a personal outpouring of your feelings. It is a tool that allows you to see yourself and your situation in a different light. By disconnecting from the situation and reading previous notes, you will see things you cannot possibly see while flooded with emotions at the time you wrote it. It will become another tool to help you "connect the dots" and recognize the path that will turn your company around.

Your turnaround "plan" will come from many different ideas, and you need to connect those ideas into one cohesive strategy. Connecting the dots is a challenging thing to do but documenting your thoughts and ideas (however improbable they may seem at the time) in a journal can help you get a 30,000-foot view. You need all the help you can get; this is a critical tool to help you along the path to your business turnaround.

Your journal will not be a public document, so do not be afraid to go deep into your thoughts while journaling; it is for your eyes only. What you write does not have to be accurate, make sense, or even be achievable. The important thing is to write. Your brain can only do so much when thinking freely, but by putting your thoughts down on paper, you access a different part of your mind that may be able to solve problems differently.

A key point here is that your specific turnaround strategies may come from a thought that you journaled a month ago, combined with something you wrote last week and another entry from this morning. While reviewing your journal, your brain will see patterns and…boom! You will discover the best turnaround strategies to help your company.

If you think you can keep all these ideas and emotions in your head, you are wrong. Be honest with yourself: if you do not write your thoughts down, would you remember an idea you had a month ago? A week ago? This morning?

Write it down. Define the problems in detail. The more you journal, the more likely you will be to go beyond the symptoms to discover the core issue.

Here is an example. At the start of Survival Frog's turnaround, I believed I had one problem to solve: low revenue that did not cover my payroll and overhead each month.

As I investigated it further and journaled, it occurred to me that my reliance on growing revenue was only the symptom of a more prominent core problem. My overhead was too high, and expenses were out of control. Furthermore, I discovered that the payroll expense was inflated because we had hired extra people to work on projects that did not bring in enough revenue to justify their employment.

Ultimately, journaling helped me realize that the problem was not that we were selling too little, but that I was over-hiring in anticipation of non-contributing projects taking off, and not keeping a close enough eye on the productivity and efficiency of my team. You can see this chain of cause and effect more clearly once you have it down in writing.

Journaling is an ongoing process of defining the company's challenges. What you think are today's biggest challenges may turn into opportunities, once you start digging in. Write down the findings of your inquiries and analysis, and revisit past journal entries often.

Getting Support

Most business owners have difficulty admitting defeat and instead keep their game face on during challenging times. People may already *come to you* for advice, so it can be tough admitting you have a problem and need help. To successfully create and execute your turnaround plan, you will need to swallow that pride and reach out to those you trust to start talking it out.

During my downturn, I just wanted to crawl under a large rock and forget about everything, and you may feel the same way. You need to get over that. I know it will feel odd to be vulnerable and ask for help from your business friends, family, and employees. It takes a village to figure out the solutions to your challenges, so open-up and talk. Then, listen.

Talking with business owner friends

I was initially hesitant to "spread the word" about my company's potential demise with my business friends, so I knew I had to push myself to reach out. I set a personal goal to meet with at least two people a week over lunch or coffee (by the way, you rarely pay for lunch when sharing how financially screwed you are).

There is something unique in talking with other business owners. It is almost like the rest of the world does not truly get you, but a fellow business owner understands. They understand the challenges in running a business and have most likely been through something like your downturn. They get it.

I had some amazing conversations with business friends, including tears, fears, and beers. It is great to get some things off your chest, but I was also able to get some solid ideas that helped me turn my business around.

Talking through turnaround ideas with someone disconnected from the problem and who does not know all the baggage associated with employees or pet projects can be very enlightening. They can sometimes see things you cannot or do not want to see.

When you are too close to the problem, it can be hard to see it for what it really is and even harder to find your way out. They say it is hard to read the label when you are inside the jar. A good talk with a smart businessperson can sometimes give you much-needed clarity on the situation.

Talk with several different types of business owners to get a wide range of feedback. A sample of those you may want to seek could include:

- people you admire
- people that admire you
- your BFFs
- people in a similar business
- people in a completely different industry
- the older, wiser entrepreneur with a ton of experience
- the new scrappy entrepreneur
- the guy you do not like much but is crazy smart
- competitors who are also struggling (although, with competitors, be strategic about the meeting and go into it with boundaries; you do not need to share everything)

In those meetings where you feel comfortable and in good company, open-up and be vulnerable. A business downturn is scary and has enormous consequences for your life and the people in your life. Many people depend on your business and are looking to you to fix it. For me, it was the perfect storm of guilt, shame, fear, and a constant feeling of uncertainty. Some of the best advice I got from business friends was on the personal side. They are your tribe.

It is tough admitting defeat, but you may as well control the narrative by approaching it as a way to learn. Be vulnerable, admit the mistakes, and look for ideas that can help create your turnaround plan.

I am a member of a business group called Entrepreneur's Organization (EO), which I joined three years before my business downturn. I can confidently say that EO, and in particular my EO Forum, was an essential resource that helped me through those difficult times. The members and friends in EO helped me with business ideas and strategies to turn around my business, but the benefits went far beyond their advice. EO helped me open-up and be vulnerable about my situation. I was able to talk through my difficult situations with people I trusted. Opening-up about my fear, guilt, and embarrassment related to my failing business helped me get through the hell I was facing. The emotional outlet was invaluable.

My business friends gave me great ideas to consider in turning around my business. But here is the catch: you most likely will not get the "one big idea" from a conversation you have. You will need to piece together different ideas, opinions, and advice from multiple sources to form your final turnaround plan. This is "connecting the dots." It is your job to process all the ideas you receive (make sure you are taking notes–did someone say journal?). Combine the best ideas, discard the bad ones, and start developing your turnaround plan.

Talking with family and friends

There is also value in talking to your family and friends who do not have businesses. This group of people may not relate to everything you are going through in the same way as your business colleagues, but they may give you a different view that will help you connect more dots.

You never know where or when those great turnaround ideas will come. It could be your cousin, your old high school friend, or maybe it was some random comment that your 80-year-old neighbor made. Someone far away from your business or business ownership can give a perspective that you have not seen before.

Of course, you need to talk with your immediate family: your spouse or partner and children. The downturn is hard on them, too. They notice your stress, that you are working longer and harder hours than usual, and that there is less money to spend as a family. While it may not be appropriate to share every monumentally bad issue (especially with younger children), you need to give them updates periodically about the high and low points.

Talking with employees

What you say to your employees and staff depends greatly on their status within the company. Partners or executive employees running the company need a different level of detail than frontline employees.

All levels of employees can be a good source of ideas in your turnaround. They have a vested interest in the company doing well.

Do not dismiss the lower-level or newer employees. Sometimes they are not as invested in the problem and may provide better out-of-the-box thinking. Give special attention to those in your customer support department who interact with your customers daily.

Talking with business professionals

This last category can get expensive, but you should not overlook experts that can add value. The most common professionals you may want to engage are Chief Financial Officers (CFOs) or other financially focused experts.

Seeking help from your attorneys is also critically important during a downturn. There could be numerous legal issues you will be working through during these challenging times. Make sure you cover your bases with proper legal representation.

Consultants and advisors, in my opinion, can produce mixed results. A good turnaround expert is worth their weight in gold, but most specialize in corporate turnarounds and may not provide as much value to small business owners. The old saying "those who can't do, teach" comes to mind when thinking about consultants, so just be sure they have relevant experience in your industry or with small business turnarounds.

Talking it out is crucial in connecting the dots and moving forward with a sound turnaround plan. Keep in mind, however, that not all the advice you get will be good. You may even get flat out wrong and lousy help. That is okay; your job is to listen and take it all in, then evaluate it alongside all your other ideas. The best idea could come from someone so far disconnected that they could see what you cannot. Maybe you will find that hidden idea that leads you down a path to solutions.

Chapter 4: Action Steps

> ➤ If you have not already, buy a new folder and start a turnaround journal. You can write about anything you want; just get it out of your head!
>
> ➤ Make a list of business owners that you know. Who can you schedule a time to talk with this week?

SECTION ONE: KEEPING YOUR SANITY

CHAPTER 5
STAYING MENTALLY AND
PHYSICALLY STRONG

Take care of your body. It's the only place you have to live. ~Jim Rohn

Taking care of your physical and mental health is crucial while going through the stress of a turnaround. Although you are busier than you have ever been, you must find the time for working out or getting fresh air and sun. Proactively caring for your physical health is vital because, as a good friend told me during my downturn, "we are going to need you when this is all over."

Balance

Above all, make sure you take time for your family and for yourself. Finding some type of balance, even if it is a 90/10 ratio of work to life, gives you 10% of your focus completely on your family and on your mental health. Find your new "balanced" life.

Strength

Getting your heart rate up and sweating has an amazing effect on your mind. Like most things, getting started is tough, but soon you will enjoy it and start to feel the benefits of more energy, sharper thinking, and greater health.

Sun

Get some direct sunlight every day, even if it is just for 10 minutes. You will be less likely to get sick and you will make sure to breathe some fresh air.

Fun

Live with passion and be curious. Even when you are having a bad day, you can find those little moments in life and have some fun. Laughter is great medicine; you need some each day. Be present, have fun.

Meditation

I started meditating a few years before my business took its sharp downturn. Meditation has proven to help my sanity and during the downturn it really paid off.

A major benefit of meditation is that it helps clear the noise out of your head. Everyone, whether they are aware of it or not, suffers from excessive mental dialogue that adds no value. It is always running in your head. Meditation helps calm that chatter and allows you to be focused.

You may be thinking, "Meditation is not for me; my mind moves too fast." If that is the case, you need meditation more than anyone.

Everyone can meditate. There are many resources including free apps you can find to help you meditate better. Personally, I have found meditation can help. If any of the following resonate with you, you may want to give meditation a try:

Being less reactive–When something goes wrong, you are less reactive to the situation and less likely to blow up. Meditation helps you witness the situation and act accordingly.

Reducing anxiety–With meditation, you have more control over stress and the anxiety that comes with it. This is a big one.

Connecting the dots–By finding a silent space in your head, you will have room to see the big picture and find clarity for solutions.

Improved health—Meditation can improve your health, which may include lowering your blood pressure and reducing your heart rate.

Enjoyment—Meditation can be so enjoyable once you get the hang of it. You work hard, so you deserve a little bliss.

Mental Health Professionals

There is no substitute for professional mental help. Keeping your sanity during a company downturn and turnaround can be tough.

Even the most energetic and positive person will struggle with the challenges ahead. Talking with friends and family can help, but only to an extent. Be on the lookout for signs of potentially life-threatening depression and desperation within yourself. I am not a licensed psychologist and can only share what worked for me. When in doubt, always get professional help. When you feel your reactions to the stress of the moment are approaching dangerous levels, reach out, and get professional advice.

Chapter 5: Action Steps
➢ How are you doing? Be sure to prioritize family, getting outside, and exercise. ➢ Are you considering meditation? Start by finding an app for your phone.

CHAPTER 6
FOCUSING ON SOLUTIONS

Identify your problems, but give your power and energy to solutions. ~Tony Robbins

As entrepreneurs, we are eternal optimists. We think we have this magic guiding light in us, and that things will always work out. Use it to your advantage but be careful with this thinking as well. You could put yourself in a state of denial, or worse, rely on "everything will work itself out," even as the world is falling apart around you.

Finding that critical balance between a positive outlook and one that acknowledges the severity of the problem is key to your mental health and for the business to survive.

You do not want to act like everything is great as your world falls apart, but you also do not want to be doom and gloom and dwell on the negatives.

I am sure you are determined to fix your company, save as many jobs as possible, and quickly get back to profitability. The actual action steps you take are critical, but having the right mental attitude is just as, if not more important.

You could have the exact step by step plan in your hands to turn your business around, but if your attitude is not in check, you may struggle to find success. You must have the right attitude and push forward with a positive mindset.

Let It Out

Before we get too far into this "froufrou positive thinking" stuff, I want to let you know it is okay to get upset. If your business is failing, then life sucks. It does! I am not going to sugarcoat this. Your baby (the company you probably started and have been growing for many years) is sick. Extremely sick. It is not fair, and you do not deserve this. So get mad. Blow up, scream at the air, get furious! It sucks, and there is no denying that it is terrifying.

I am usually a very calm guy, yet during my own business downturn, I had several "episodes." I screamed, I cried, and basically lost my shit.

Let it out. Go for it. But make sure you get it out of your system because the other 98% of the time, you need to keep a cool head and focus on the solutions to your issues in a calm and controlled manner.

What Your Employees Need to See

Your team is looking to you for leadership during these difficult times. They are looking to you for confidence in a plan that will fix the company. It is the cool-headed leader with a plan that can save the day.

While you do not want to always be a sobbing mess in front of your employees, I do think it is healthy to show some emotions. It shows you are human, that you care, and this is an exceedingly difficult process for you, especially when dealing with layoffs. However, for the vast majority of time, your employees will look to you for confidence and a plan forward.

Asking the Right Questions

A big part of keeping your sanity during such an emotional and challenging time of your life is how you look at your problems and the questions you ask.

Here are a few:

- How could this become a good thing in a few years?

- What can I learn from this and how will this help me become a better business owner in the future?
- What is the core issue at hand?
- What is the story I am telling myself about this downturn?

You Will Find What You Are Actively Looking For

I am sure that at some point in your life, you have purchased a new car. Ever notice how you start seeing so many vehicles of the same make and model? The part of your brain called the reticular activating system (RAS) now picks up on every similar car in sight. Suddenly, they are everywhere. Were they everywhere before this? Yes, but you did not notice. Your RAS was not picking up on it.

The same thing happens if you are looking for opportunities or solutions to your problems. Your RAS will suddenly start to find them for you. Amazing things will happen when you focus on the solutions, not the problems.

Is your RAS finding more problems for you to work on, or is it searching for opportunities? It is going to find something either way, and so you might as well be intentional with your thoughts.

If you are only focusing on how bad things are, you are likely to get more of those bad things in your life. The universe will always give you more of what you spend the most time focusing on, so be careful where you are putting your energy.

I am not saying to ignore the bad things. I am suggesting you should spend 20% of the time focused on the problem, and 80% on solutions.

Chapter 6: Action Steps

- ➤ Make a list of "big idea" questions you can ask yourself. Schedule time every week to think about and journal your answers.
- ➤ Identify the challenge, then spend 80% of your time thinking of potential solutions.

SECTION ONE: KEEPING YOUR SANITY

CHAPTER 7
REALIZING MOMENTUM
IS YOUR FRIEND

Perfection is the enemy of profitability. *~Mark Cuban*

During Survival Frog's turnaround, it felt like we were flying a broken plane hurtling towards the ground. We were feverishly trying to fix the plane while at the same time, keeping it in the air and taking care of normal day-to-day operations. There were constant "fires" on board, and every time we had put one out, another crisis would emerge. There were so many difficult decisions and a never-ending list of demanding conversations that had to happen. But we never gave up, and each day we showed up ready to fight another day.

This constant state of action helped us all stay sane, especially me. I knew there was a good chance we could end up crashing the plane and forced to close the business, but I was not going down without a fight.

Progress, Not Perfection

When you are frozen with fear and unsure which way to turn, sometimes the best remedy is to just start. Even if you do not yet have a completed turnaround plan mapped out, you can start working towards a solution today. Action leads to more action, which can create the momentum of change that your business needs.

Do not get hung up on perfection. Even if you make the wrong or a less than perfect decision, it is better to create that momentum. Being paralyzed with fear and not making any decisions is far worse than pushing forward with the possibility of mistakes along the way.

You do not have to create the definitive absolute final plan now; you just need to start writing down your ideas and coming up with a checklist of tasks. Perfection is the killer of profits, and it is the death of a company that needs to act quickly.

Making Decisions With Only 70% Of the Information

During the turnaround, you will rarely have all the information you would like. If you are waiting for the green light or the definitive answer that says, "This is exactly what you need to do," you can just get over it–that is not going to happen. There are too many moving parts during the downturn for you to nail anything down 100%. Quite often, leaders need to make quick decisions, with only part of the information available. You are just not going to get 100% of the information before you make a decision.

It may seem that 70% of the information is not nearly enough, but you have something more. You also have your gut. I am sure you have been running this business for a while; you have been in the industry for quite some time, and this is not your first rodeo. You have seen all the moving parts for a few years now, so your gut will often lead you in the right direction. 70%, along with your gut, will often be enough.

During my turnaround, I found that making the wrong decision is often better than not making any decision. Sometimes it is okay to make a wrong decision, even one that you may have to reverse and correct later. Making small decisions brings movement and action, which is more important than getting it right.

Designing the First Steps

One of the benefits of taking action is that you can feel the momentum in the air. Momentum is your friend. If you can take some baby steps, they lead to bigger steps, leading to even more significant action. Soon enough, you will start to see results. Those first initial steps are sometimes the hardest, but they can also be the most important.

Think about when you first start going to the gym. The first couple of times are by far the hardest. By the tenth time, you cannot stay out of the gym because it becomes a habit. However, those first few times are the worst.

The same applies to your turnaround. The first few steps are tricky because you have no momentum. Merely acting, even if it is not the perfect action, is movement. That movement creates momentum. After that, the next steps get a little easier.

Being Proactive, Not Reactive

Many people in stressful situations live a very reactive life. A reactive life is one that is continuously moving with the wind. You can start to feel like you spend your whole day putting out fires, with little control over the direction you are heading.

In a reactive state, you can bounce from one project to another, with a hyperactive problem-solving style. While there are certainly going to be times where you must jump in and react to situations, you need to find a way to be proactive at least part of your day. Maybe, in the beginning, it is ten minutes of proactive time per day. To continue with the gym metaphor, perhaps just getting to the gym, walking in, and doing a ten-minute workout is okay. You need to start somewhere. Find the time to be strategic with your turnaround.

At one point during my turnaround, I remember thinking that "I wasn't playing to win, I was playing not to lose." This thought helped remind me that the turnaround was more than just trying to save the sinking ship; it was about creating a better and faster ship that could take me to new and uncharted waters.

Make sure you have a portion of every day that is proactive. That means you are sitting down and journaling and getting ideas out of your head. Even if only five minutes is available today, write something. There must be a dozen or more "proactive" projects you can focus on that will get you further down the path of your turnaround.

Documenting the Plan

Confusion is common during unpredictable times, so if you do not know what direction to go next, you are not alone. When this happens, you need to get whatever is bothering you out of your head and into your journal. Whether it is on your computer or handwritten, get it out. Even if you sit down unsure what you are going to write, just start writing. Allow yourself to write pages and pages of notes if you need to. Get it out of your head.

Maybe at first, it is just all the emotions you are feeling. Put them down on paper. Right now, your thoughts and ideas do not even need to be rational. Get it out of your head.

What you write down is only for you, so no one else is going to see this. A month from now, you can rip it up and throw it away (although I suggest you do not).

If you document what is going on in your mind every day, you will start to see patterns. There is something magical about having your thoughts available in a written form in front of you so you can review them readily. As you review previous journal entries, you can start to see patterns and organize those thoughts a little bit better. Then you can share some parts of a turnaround idea with other people who can help with feedback.

Every turnaround plan begins with a basic strategy, and eventually, it becomes clearer and more focused. It takes time and only comes once you have been at it for a while. Your turnaround strategies will not all come at once; it is a process that you need to go through. Start now, so over time your plans begin to take shape, and you start to see results.

Starting Your Turnaround Process Now

As mentioned several times already, the faster you act, the sooner you see results. I have also found the opposite is true: the slower you move, the more likely it is that the problem will get much worse. Do not put this off another day; you need to start your business turnaround now. Do not live in denial or think the problem will go away by itself. Acknowledge the situation in its full ugliness and start on fixing it now.

Picking up this book is an excellent start toward your turnaround success but keep searching for the answers. Listen to podcasts that focus on small business strategies. Google the heck out of everything: all ideas, all potential solutions. Ask others for help, seek guidance from those you trust, and keep asking questions until you find your answers. When the student is ready, the teacher will appear.

Chapter 7: Action Steps

Grab your journal and then consider the following:

➤ What areas are you putting too much time into making perfect? How can you move faster, even if you only have 70% of the information needed?
➤ List out five easy tasks that you can complete by tomorrow. Cut a few expenses and set up a few meetings. Get that momentum kick started.
➤ Review some previous journal entries you have made. Look at your challenges with fresh eyes and start to connect the dots with your turnaround plan.

SECTION ONE: KEEPING YOUR SANITY

CHAPTER 8
WELCOME ADVERSITY

All the adversity I've had in my life, all my troubles and obstacles, have strengthened me. You may not realize it when it happens, but a kick in the teeth may be the best thing in the world for you. ~Walt Disney

Success feels like growth, but in reality, failure and challenges are what makes you expand the most. You learn from your successes, but you learn a lot more from your failures. Welcome adversity.

Your turnaround is a gift, and that gift is the new person you become, and the improved company you will have.

From fire and destruction comes new life. No one has ever enjoyed the ride, but most people are appreciative after a difficult journey is over.

The challenges you experience throughout your downturn and turnaround will push you and cause you to grow. You will learn what you are made of, which will help you to carry much confidence into your next challenging situation.

I do not expect you to be happy while you are going through this downturn. It sucks, and I get that. But underneath it all, you should be looking for how this test will help you in the long run. What good will come from these challenging times? How much smarter and better will you become once you get through it?

The affirmation I came back to time and again during my downturn is, at the risk of repeating myself:

"Bad things don't happen to me; they happen for me. For me to be stronger, smarter, and..." You fill in the blank.

You often cannot see the good when you are going through difficult times, so some of this advice is going to have to be taken on faith. Have faith that when this is all over, you will have a better, more profitable business. If the worst-case scenario happens and you lose your business, you will be wiser when you start your next journey.

The Result is a Better Company

A business that survives a turnaround is far better than it was before. Your company's efficiency level goes through the roof, your expenses are low, and your margins are tweaked and on-point.

If you take an inefficient company and increase sales, it will grow. However, profits may not increase substantially, and often the problems just get larger.

Alternatively, if you take a company that has been through a turnaround and gotten to the other side and then increase sales, it just does amazing things! It grows faster, better, and is more profitable than an inefficiently run business. If you hope for a big client, or the market to return, wish for these things to happen after you have a company that has survived a turnaround.

The Result is a Better You

On the personal side, anyone who has been through difficult times and challenges in their lives tends to appreciate life a bit more afterward. They have a better outlook.

We see it all the time with people who have near-death experiences. They turn a new leaf; they have a new spirit. They come back with renewed energy, and that is what you will have when you almost lose your business but come out on the other side.

The new appreciation of life in general, and indeed, your business, means you can do more with less, and you can approach it with a great attitude. Adversity builds character, and it brings out the best in people. Have the faith that when you are done, there is a gift. There is a better company, and a better you.

Continuing Your Mindset Work

The mental work we talked about in this section never ends. It is not like keeping your sanity or taking care of your mental game is over when you finish reading this chapter. You never finish. The mental work is an ongoing thing throughout your turnaround, starting right now. Every step, every day, every decision will come back to you having the mental strength to get through the turnaround.

You are going to have good days and bad days. One day you feel great, and then boom, you may hit another wall. This mental up and down is your new norm for a while. Getting your head on straight once does not mean it is permanently straight. It just means it is on straight today. I had to come back to these strategies over and over and over. It will never go away because it is a part of the entrepreneurial journey.

When you have gotten some of the chatter out of your head, through discussion, meditation, journaling, and planning turnaround ideas, only then will you be ready for the next big step.

The next step involves looking into the financial side of things. You cannot come up with a turnaround plan without the financials. Are you ready?

Then let's do it!

Chapter 8: Action Steps

> ➢ How could this uncomfortable and scary downturn actually become a good thing in a few years? Write your answer in your turnaround journal.
> ➢ What are you grateful for today (both business and personal)? Write them down.

SECTION ONE: KEEPING YOUR SANITY

SECTION TWO
MASTERING YOUR
FINANCIALS

The answer is always found within the financials.
~Byron

As head of your company, your responsibility is to turn your downturn into a turnaround as quickly as possible. You will be faced with important and difficult decisions almost every day. In order to make the right decisions, you must have the correct financial information in front of you.

I have good news and bad news regarding your business turnaround. The good news is that you already have the solution to finding your successful turnaround strategy, and it is right in front of you.

The bad news is that solution is buried within your financial books. If you are at all like I was when my downturn hit, you will need to learn a lot to make sense of that financial information—and fast!

Before my downturn, I thought I had a good handle on my finances. I read the reports provided by my accounting department at the end of each month and could determine how well the company was doing.

I freely admit I was not analyzing the numbers as I should have been. Since we were profitable and had cash in the bank, I thought that was enough.

During my downturn, I rapidly learned that a quick review of the monthly P&L for net profit and margins is not enough.

Your company needs to change and change rapidly. To know what areas need changing and improving, you must determine the key performance indicators (KPI) and learn how to track their history, as well as forecasting your way to better company health.

I am not a financial expert, and I have no formal training in it. Honestly, accounting was just something I left up to my accounting manager once per month and my certified public accountant (CPA) once a year at tax time.

When the losses started showing up on my P&L, I knew I needed additional help analyzing the cause of the problems. I knew lower revenue was the elephant in the room trampling all over my company, but there was more to the story than just lower revenue. There always is.

In this book, I will show you how to make sense of your finances and how to use that information to create your own turnaround plan and get back to profitability.

I will help you avoid the slow learning curve I experienced by sharing what worked (and what did not work) and the strategies and tactics I used to turn around my company.

Mastering your finances comes down to three main points, each of which I will guide you through in detail:

- Managing your cash runway
- Understanding changes in your historic P&L
- Forecasting different turnaround strategies

I will clearly explain each of those principles soon, but before continuing, I suspect that we need to address that voice that is screaming inside your head.

SECTION TWO: MASTERING YOUR FINANCIALS

CHAPTER 9
OVERCOMING YOUR
FEAR OF FINANCIALS

Your numbers are talking... are you listening? ~Greg Crabtree

I can hear you from here. "But Byron, I'm not a financial expert! I can't do this!"

It is easy to be intimidated. Most accountants present financial reports in a way that is difficult to read, making it harder to see the big picture.

You *can* master your financials, and you must. The secret is to present the financials, so it is easy for your entrepreneur mind to read and understand. Often this means creating a layout that is ultra-simple and easy to manipulate.

Entrepreneurs are visionaries who love to grow businesses. Although you may feel you can put aside the financials and just focus on selling more, your financials are the exact place you must focus during a turnaround.

To determine what has gone wrong with your business and what areas you need to fix, you first need to dive into the numbers.

Take this challenge as your calling, to go to the next level of entrepreneurship. Master your financials. You must do this.

Simplify the Data

Innovators and visionaries are wired differently than accountants. You need to read the numbers in a way that makes sense to you.

As entrepreneurs, our minds are particularly good at seeing trends and patterns. We can connect the dots. We understand the big picture. That is what your financial statements can do for you when presented in the right way. Your goal is to change how you read your financials so that you can easily see the bigger picture.

Ask your accounting manager or bookkeeper to make the financial reports simple. Instead of showing 100 lines on your P&L, ask him or her to consolidate it down to 10 or fewer categories. This will allow you to see what areas of your company are in trouble and unpack an item later to find the solutions.

Another game-changer for me was converting my reports to percentages versus just dollar amounts. A P&L made up of only dollar amounts starts to look like nothing more than a bunch of confusing numbers.

To determine the percentage for each section of your P&L, simply divide each number by the gross revenue. This will help you see the correlation between the numbers when the revenue levels change. When you focus on the ratios behind the numbers you can start to see trends. We will discuss this further in Chapter 11.

Before we dive into these strategies in more depth, I want to share one more critical piece of advice. When it comes to "who" oversees picking apart the financials and finding the solutions, there is only one answer. You must lead the way in mastering your financials.

You will have help from bookkeepers or your accounting manager. You may even have help from a fractional CFO or a financial Controller along the way. However, under no circumstances can you just turn over this task to them and not focus your time on the financials.

The owner of the business or active CEO leading the turnaround must be the one who is ultimately in charge of learning from the financials. The better you become at interpreting the financials, the better chance you have for a successful turnaround.

Cleaning Up the Financials

As you dig into your financials, you will start exposing weaknesses in your accounting department. Where you once trusted the monthly financials you now second guess everything.

It is common to find inconsistencies in how reporting is done and even glaring mistakes along the way. It is frustrating and it makes the turnaround planning even harder, but it is common. To make things worse, delays in getting monthly financial reports is downright painful.

Work through those issues and continue to strive for more accurate financial books. However, do not let inaccurate or delayed data slow down your turnaround planning. Even with inconsistent data, you must start formulating a plan now.

Yes, You Can Do This!

You know your business and your market. By comparing the ratios from when your company was healthy to the current dire situation, you will start to see trends.

Although a significant portion of your time and focus will be spent understanding and mastering the elements of your P&L Statements, the *first* thing you need to do is figure out your cash runway.

Chapter 9: Action Steps

➤ What is your current level of financial savviness? Where do you expect to be once this turnaround is over? Document this in your journal.

➤ What is the current condition of your financial books (accuracy and readability)? What do you expect the financials to look like once this turnaround is over? Document your notes.

SECTION TWO: MASTERING YOUR FINANCIALS

CHAPTER 10
DETERMINING YOUR
CASH RUNWAY

It was as if we were driving along, watching only the speedometer, when in fact we were running out of gas. ~Michael Dell

Your cash runway tells you how long you can operate your business before you run out of money. Knowing this number is critical to your survival and something you need to focus on almost every day.

It is a simple calculation. How much money do you have in the bank? Divide that by your weekly cash losses, and that will tell you if you have six months, or two months, or two weeks before you run out of cash.

For example, Table 10-01 shows that you only have 3 weeks runway before your company is out of cash. Running out of cash is bad, but running out of cash unexpectantly is really, really bad. Forecasting your cash runway is a critical part of your turnaround strategy.

Your Cash in the Bank	$50,000
Weekly Losses	$15,000
Cash Runway ($50,000/$15,000)	3.3 Weeks

Table 10-01

Three weeks cash runway is a scary scenario to be in, but it gives you the clarity on what needs to be done, and how fast.

What if you were able to cut $7,500 out of your weekly overhead budget? You would still be losing money, but this could help extend your cash runway, giving you more time to execute your turnaround plan.

I know, I hear you saying, "that's impossible, I can't cut any more money from my budget!" That is exactly what I said in the early part of my business downturn, but I did find creative ways to cut my expenses (more on cutting expenses in Section 4).

What would it look like if we cut expenses? What if weekly cash losses went from $15,000 per week to $7,500?

Your Cash in the Bank	$50,000
Weekly Losses	$7,500
Cash Runway ($50,000/$7,500)	6.6 Weeks

Table 10-02

Now we are at 6 ½ weeks cash runway! That could give you the extra time you need to make some big changes. But here is where a lot of entrepreneurs get caught up.

This opportunity to extend your cash runway has a short window of opportunity. The 6 ½ weeks is only possible if you make those cuts in expenses today. If the cost reduction happens in 2 weeks, your runway will be significantly shorter than it is now.

The longer you wait, the shorter that runway gets, and you put your business in greater danger. You must act now.

Once the money is gone, it cannot come back. That is why you must be open to cutting fast and deep and *do it now* because that will extend your cash runway.

Weekly Cashflow Forecast

One of the best pieces of turnaround advice I received came as I was sitting in Starbucks with my good friend Zack DeLisa.

I felt lightheaded as I sipped my coffee. My business was in a complete tailspin, and I was scared. I knew things were bad, but honestly, I did not yet know how bad.

I wondered each day if I would walk into the office to discover the game was over, and we would have to shut things down. I pictured my Accounting Manager running up to me with the look of fear in his eyes and breaking the bad news to me. Not knowing my cash runway was a very uneasy feeling, and I just was not finding the answers in my P&L.

As I confided in my friend this fear of not knowing when the game would be over, he leaned in and made a powerful suggestion that helped save my sanity. Zack suggested I stop trying to manage my business on the P&L and start using a cashflow forecast instead.

Zack had 20+ years of financial experience in helping businesses during good and bad times. He went on to explain how the P&L is great for monthly planning and overarching strategies (needed to create your turnaround plan). However, for crisis management and knowing when the ride may end abruptly, you need a cashflow forecast.

At the time, I did not have a cashflow forecast, and I was managing the business on the P&L. The P&L was showing massive losses and painted the picture that we were doomed.

However, once Zack helped me to build out my cashflow forecast, I started looking at cash instead of profit. I also realized that we could still have money in the bank even though we were experiencing heavy losses. Because my company sold physical products, we were able to survive off the inventory we had in the warehouse. We had large losses on the P&L, but we still had money in the bank.

The Best Sleeping Pill

During my downturn, there were many, many sleepless nights. Would we be able to make payroll this week? How about next week, or the week after? It was not knowing that was the hardest part, but the cashflow forecast gave me clarity around our cash runway so I could always see how much time we had left. The cashflow forecast gave me a window into the future.

I knew things were bad and I figured we would probably be forced to shut down the business at some point. However, my cashflow forecast showed I had at least 3 weeks cash runway. Although the 4th week was unknown, I did have confidence we could survive 3 more weeks. I knew I may go out of business, but it was not going to happen in the next few weeks!

That allowed me to disconnect, relax and get some much-needed sleep. Having the confidence that it was not all going to implode on me tomorrow allowed me to sleep. The cashflow forecast is the best sleeping pill available.

The downturn situation was still terrifying, but at least I had a few weeks to keep swinging and trying to figure things out.

Sample Cashflow Forecast

The concept behind the cashflow forecast is simple. Organizing all your cash outlays and forecasting future revenues is where the challenge is.

Table 10-03 on page 92 displays a sample spreadsheet. It starts with the beginning balance in your bank. Just login to your bank and grab the opening balance each Monday.

Then you add the forecasted revenue you expect to see each week. Be conservative with sales revenue and have high confidence in collecting accounts receivable before you add this inflow number. It can be difficult to pin down the revenue forecast but even a wrong number is better than not having this spreadsheet built out. Each week, you will get better at forecasting the money coming in the door.

For the next step you can get help from your bookkeeper and determine the timing of all cash payments, or outflows, you make throughout the month. Get the timing right (when the money leaves the bank account) and build out the next few months. This will be eye opening as you see all the areas the money flows out of your company.

Finally, some quick math; beginning balance plus cash inflows minus outflows. The number you are left with is your forecasted ending balance. Next week you will look at your bank balance and see how close you were to this number.

Table 10-03 on page 92 is a simplified version of the cashflow forecast.

The table depicts a 6 ½ week runway before running out of cash. Although you know you still have some difficult decisions ahead, you have confidence that you will have cash to cover your obligations for at least the next month. This gives you a little time to execute your amazing turnaround plan.

Table 10-03 is a very simplified example, and your cashflow forecast is going to be 50 lines or more long with expected cash outlays. Each bill, invoice and amount due needs to find its way to this spreadsheet, preferably several weeks or months before the bill is actually paid out.

It may take some effort, but once you have your cashflow forecast dialed in, you should have a noticeably clear picture of the next three to four weeks.

However, the cashflow forecast gets a little blurry after four weeks, and this is to be expected. It is hard to predict every expense and revenue levels that far out. You are most interested in the next three to four weeks to make sure you have cash in the bank to meet your obligations. The goal is to be accurate several months ahead, but you just need the next month to be spot on accurate.

	Current Week	Week 2	Week 3	Week 4	Week 5	Week 6	Week 7
Beginning Balance	$50,000	$35,000	$34,000	$31,000	$31,000	$6,000	$10,000
Cash inflow	+$20,000	+$25,000	+$20,000	+$25,000	+$10,000	+$30,000	+$10,000
Cash out: Rent	-$10,000				-$10,000		
Cash out: Marketing		-$2,000		-$2,000		-$2,000	
Cash out: Software		-$3,000				-$3,000	
Cash out: Payroll	-$15,000	-$15,000	-$15,000	-$15,000	-$15,000	-$15,000	-$15,000
Cash out: Other	-$10,000	-$6,000	-$8,000	-$8,000	-$10,000	-$6,000	-$7,000
Ending Balance	**$35,000**	**$34,000**	**$31,000**	**$31,000**	**$6,000**	**$10,000**	**-$2,000**

Table 10-03

Cash is King

Cash is the most valuable asset you have in crisis management. Cash helps you keep the lights on while you spend your limited time turning around your business. The more cash runway you have, the more time you have to fix the problems.

Cash in the bank not only gives you more time it also opens additional options. The longer it takes you to cut costs, the less cash you will have in the bank and fewer options you will have to save the business. Less cash means less time. The faster you act to lower your expenses, or increase revenue, the longer your cash runway will be.

Note: the cashflow forecast has little to do with the profitability of your company. It focuses only on the cash movements. For profit, you must look to your P&L.

For example, cash inflow is not necessarily revenue. You could pull $20,000 from your line of credit, and it will show as inflow cash sitting in your bank, but that's not revenue you will find on your P&L, and it is certainly not going to be seen as profit.

Also, note that expected cash outflows do not include purchases made on credit. Only when you pay off that credit with your cash will it show up on the cashflow forecast. We are only looking at the cash moving in and out of the business.

Who Creates the Cashflow Forecast?

It was mentioned before but it is worth repeating that you must lead this effort in learning from the financials and the cashflow runway.

You will undoubtedly get some of the information you need from your accountant, but it is critical that you do not just delegate the cashflow forecast responsibility. You will need to be fully engaged in not only analyzing but also creating your cashflow forecast spreadsheet and making sure it is accurate each Monday.

As the entrepreneur and the owner of your company, you know all the moving parts. You may know about an expense coming up that the accountant does not have on their radar. You must keep your finger on the pulse of this document. The business is your baby, so protect it by keeping cash in the bank. Get involved and make sure you have confidence in the numbers.

Timing of Large Purchases

Doing this exercise every Monday morning shows you the areas you need to focus on *urgently* in the coming weeks. If you see a negative number coming up on your cashflow forecast that tells you checks are going to start bouncing and people will not get paid.

How are you going to fix this upcoming crisis? The first answer is increasing revenue or decreasing expenses, both of which I will cover in detail. There is another option which is to change the timing of the money coming in or going out.

The cashflow forecast will let you see into the future, so you have time to react to problems coming up in one to two weeks.

You may be able to delay payments owed by making a few phone calls and asking for more time. You may be able to speed up accounts receivable and collect on some cash early.

My cashflow forecast saved my butt many times. At one point, we were planning on ordering another container of physical products costing $40,000. When I put the figures for the purchase into my cashflow forecast it created a negative balance a few weeks later.

When I looked in the bank, I could see I had the cash that day, but if I made the purchase, I would be out of cash in 2 weeks. Only the cashflow forecast can give you this type of insight into your business.

This knowledge allowed me to do two things. I reduced that $40,000 purchase to $30,000 by removing a few products, and I bumped the purchase back two weeks. I decided it would be okay to run low on some products until we had the cash we needed two weeks down the road. The forecast helped me to head off a cash crisis that was coming before it happened. If I had only looked in my bank account to see if I had $40,000, I would have made that purchase and we would have been in big trouble.

Your Cashflow Forecast Will Never be Perfect

If you think that you can get your forecast 100% dialed in, forget it, it will always be off. Your first few weeks or even months may be very inaccurate as you gather information on your revenues and expenses. Your goal is to make it less "wrong" the longer you work the forecast.

If you can get within 10% accuracy, you are doing great. At first, you may be off by 50%, but even that gives you information that can help you to tweak the forecast so that the next week, maybe you are only off by 40%. Then 30%. Your goal is to get better and better over time. But it will never be 100% perfect. And that is okay–progress, not perfection.

Increase Your Cash Position

Once you have some insight into your cash runway, it is time to improve your cash standing.

Some strategies can significantly increase your cash position in a short amount of time. These ideas may sound simple, but do not dismiss them. Increasing your cash position is powerful, and will help lengthen your cash runway, giving you time to implement your turnaround plan.

Work with vendors to slow down accounts payable

Many vendors, if asked, will work with you when you are in cash distress. Put yourself in their shoes. They would prefer that you pay them late instead of not at all. If you run out of cash and go out of business, they will not get paid.

As the owner, I would recommend you personally reach out to the vendors, especially on your larger accounts. Explain your situation and assure them with confidence that you have a plan to move forward and get the company through this. Ask for more time. Maybe you suggest three months deferral on payments or smaller payments over more time. Look for incentives for the vendor to make the concessions, such as removing volume discounts or rebates.

If the vendor is a one-off relationship and you are not worried about future business with them, you may be able to negotiate a sizable discount on the money owed. By painting a picture of despair, you may be able to offer 50% or less, and the vendor may take the money to avoid the possibility of getting nothing later.

Collect accounts receivable faster

This strategy is the counterpart of paying your payables slower. Again, for your best and highest dollar customer, you as the owner need to work with the clients directly. Their payment is the lifeline for your business, and therefore you are the best person to collect it.

If you are in a recessionary economy, your customers may be hurting, and now you are on the other side of the fence. Offer payment plans or give discounts to pay in cash up front. Would you prefer to take 50% of what a customer owes you now or risk not getting anything in the future? If you are looking for cash, you want to take the money now.

Liquidate

This strategy works exceptionally well if you have physical inventory. As part of my turnaround plan, we went from 550 products in our product line to 170. We were no longer actively marketing 380 products but still had all that inventory in our warehouse. We needed the cash, so we discounted the price and sold the discontinued items quickly.

We did not make a profit from the liquidation, and hence the P&L showed losses from this strategy. However, by selling off our inventory of those 380 products, we got much-needed cash in the door and increased our cash runway substantially.

Since we had cut those products from our product line, we did not have to repurchase them, so it was cash in the bank. If we had liquidated the 170 products we were keeping, we would have had to restock, and the cash gain would have only been temporary. We did not have to replace the 380 discontinued products, so that helped extend our cash runway.

You may also have unused equipment or other assets that you could sell to raise some cash. Everything is on the table.

Credit

There is the option to take out a short-term loan that may provide the runway needed to act on your turnaround plan.

However, a word of caution is to make sure you have a solid turnaround plan and a P&L forecast that you are confident in and shows profitability soon.

A short-term loan may make sense when you expect to be in a better position in the future, but you do not want just to borrow money to throw at a problem. That merely makes it more painful three months down the road when the money did not help, and you still must go out of business.

Forgivable grants

Through the 2020 COVID downturn, the government helped small businesses with Payroll Protection Program forgivable loans and attractive Economic Injury Disaster Loans as a part of the CARES Act. During national downturns, it is common for the government to step in and help businesses, but you must be aggressive to apply for this help.

Chapter 10: Action Steps

➢ Create a list of every expense your company has had over the last 12 months, then group the reoccurring bills.

➢ Create your cashflow forecast in a spreadsheet by predicting when each upcoming "cash-out" event will take place (bills, inventory orders, etc.). Work towards making the first three weeks as accurate as possible.

➢ What are the five things you can do to improve your cash position, thus increasing your cash runway?

CHAPTER 11
MASTERING YOUR P&L
STATEMENTS

Revenue is vanity, profit is sanity, and cash flow is reality. ~Unknown

Your turnaround plan is dependent on having an adequate cash runway to get you headed in the right direction, but that just buys you time. You will find the long-term solution to your downturn within the Profit & Loss statement, or P&L.

Cash vs Profits

As mentioned previously, an important distinction in accounting is the difference between "cash" and "profits." While they may sound similar, they are quite different.

While some companies run their financials on a cash basis (meaning income or expense are realized when the cash hits or leaves the bank account), most operate on an accrual basis. In accrual accounting, you can only record an expense when you incur it, not when you pay it. So, you can see there would be a big difference between your cashflow forecast and your actual profits seen on the P&L.

Table 11-01 shows an example. If you pay for insurance once per year, you will take the cash hit on the first month but will not expense the full amount on month one. Instead, you will divide the amount by 12 months and expense it each month over the next year.

	Cashflow Forecast	P&L Accrual Basis
Insurance Payment	-$12,000	-$1,000 (per month x 12)

Table 11-01

Another example is the purchase of inventory. If you buy $40,000 worth of product, it is not an expense on the P&L

until you sell it. However, it does result in $40,000 cash flowing out of your checking account, as shown on Table 11-02:

	Cashflow Forecast	P&L Accrual Basis
Inventory Purchase	-$40,000	-$0 (until sold)

Table 11-02

One last example is when you use credit to pay for an expense. If you have $5,000 in marketing expenses and you charge this amount to your credit card you will find this expense on this month's P&L. However, you did not spend any of your cash, so this will not affect your cashflow forecast, or at least not until you pay off the credit card or make a minimum payment.

	Cashflow Forecast	P&L Accrual Basis
Expenses Charged to Credit Card	-$0	-$5,000

Table 11-03

The P&L statement shows profit, not cash, and is a more accurate measure of your company's long-term health. Cash does not equal profit.

Chunk it Down and Look at Percentages

Most P&Ls have dozens of line items and are obnoxiously complicated. By simplifying the P&L into 5-10 categories you will start to see the big picture and where changes are required. When you see areas of concern (or opportunities), you can unpack the condensed numbers to take a closer look.

For example, if you have 15 different line items under your marketing expenses, you can combine them into one marketing category. If you discover your marketing budget has increased to unhealthy levels, you can unpack that area to investigate the cause.

The simplified P&L is more manageable. It all fits on one screen, and your brain can process it more readily.

Once you have analyzed your simplified or condensed categories on the P&L, grab a box of tissues, wipe away the tears, and get ready to find the solutions.

I recommend collecting data from three or four different historical periods, such as when your business was booming, when things started trending downward, and now, when things are caving in.

Your simplified P&L may look like Table 11-04 below. It is helpful but may still be hard to analyze because the dollar amounts often do not tell the full story.

	The Good Ole' Days	Downward Trending	Current Meltdown
Gross Revenue	$500,000	$380,000	$250,000
Cost of Goods Sold	-$225,000	-$200,000	-$175,000
Marketing & Sales	-$50,000	-$45,000	-$40,000
Labor	-$50,000	-$45,000	-$40,000
Operating Expenses	-$40,000	-$40,000	-$40,000
Net Profit	**$135,000**	**$50,000**	**-$45,000**

Table 11-04

When looking at Table 11-04, you can see that gross revenue is falling, and you may conclude that you have also reduced your expenses to match that trend. However, this simply is not the case.

When you convert the dollar amounts to percentages, you will see a much different picture, as shown on Table 11-05 on page 106. Say you had $500,000 in revenue and $50,000 labor cost. Your labor cost is 10% of revenue (divide $500,000 by $50,000). That was in the good ol' days. Today, the labor cost is lower, but the $40,000 you are spending is now a whopping 16% of your revenue, which is a 60% increase in your labor as a percentage, a big red flag.

	The Good Ole' Days	%	Downward Trending	%	Current Meltdown	%
Gross Revenue	$500,000		$380,000		$250,000	
Cost of Goods Sold	-$225,000	45%	-$200,000	53%	-$175,000	70%
Marketing & Sales	-$50,000	10%	-$45,000	12%	-$40,000	16%
Labor	-$50,000	10%	-$45,000	12%	-$40,000	16%
Operating Expenses	-$40,000	8%	-$40,000	11%	-$40,000	16%
Net Profit	$135,000		$50,000		-$45,000	

Table 11-05

Without analyzing the percentages, you are not able to see the problem. Percentages are simple and straightforward allowing you to connect the dots and spot the trends.

By simplifying your P&L and comparing percentages of each expense, you can better analyze what is causing the downturn and how to create your own turnaround plan.

Comparing Your P&L Between Yesterday and Today

Let's look at the P&L in Table 11-05, now that we have percentages to help us. What initially looked like you were lowering costs as the revenue was dropping now paints a different picture.

The cost of goods sold (COGS) is potentially the most significant issue here. It went from 50% up to 70% when comparing the costs to the gross revenue the goods created. That is a big red flag, and you may not be able to see this issue without using percentages to compare month over month. Something has changed and further investigation is needed here.

Marketing is usually the last place I look to cut, but there are areas you can optimize to make sure your marketing dollars go further. Based on the percentages moving higher, your marketing is not working. Further investigation is needed here.

As mentioned before, the labor costs are also going in the wrong direction, and despite reducing or laying off 20% of your staff, it was not enough. As a percentage, your costs went from 10% up to 16%.

Operating costs are fixed, right? So how can you lower those expenses? Believe me; there are ways. You may still see your overhead percentage moving higher as revenue drops (this is a hard trend to fight), but you can certainly control some of these expenses to minimize the negative impact.

Using percentages to compare the good ol' days with today will often result in surprising discoveries. As a company grows its revenue, the percentages start to show signs of weakness. Just looking at the net profit number will not reveal what is causing these problems.

For example, as you add more items to your product line, the gross margin (revenue minus cost of goods sold) may slowly start to creep downward. It is usually so slow that you cannot see it happening, especially if you are only looking at the dollar amounts. When you convert your P&L reports to percentages, you see that margins are getting worse.

When you compare three or five different P&L monthly reports against each other, you will start seeing the trends. Doing this type of analysis in any area that appears to be weakening will help you determine what has changed between when times were good and now.

Once the problem areas have been identified, you can start taking steps to get the percentages back to where they were when profits were strong. Work on increasing gross margins and reducing expenses or labor to pre-downturn percentages. This is how your turnaround plan will start to take shape and you will see the path ahead of you.

Contrary to what you might believe, a decrease in revenue is *not the only thing* that has caused your company's downturn. It is usually just one of the several problems that you will find under the hood once you start looking. That is why increasing revenue does not really solve the underlying problem; it just covers it up for the present.

Chapter 11: Action Steps

➤ Ask your bookkeeper to collect the last six months of P&L reports. On one spreadsheet list each month in a simplified format, so you only have 5 to 10 categories to review. Add in percentages to make it easier to see trends. Digest this document, ask questions, and dig in!

➤ What has changed from when you were profitable to now? Hint: look at the percentages, not the dollar amounts.

SECTION TWO: MASTERING YOUR FINANCIALS

CHAPTER 12
FORECASTING P&L SCENARIOS

*A good forecaster is not smarter than everyone else,
he merely has his ignorance better organized.*
~Anonymous

Once armed with some historic P&L trends, your next step
is to look forward. Similar to how you used previous
expenses to create the cashflow forecast, you can use
historic P&L data to help you predict future profitability
under various scenarios. You can build out different
turnaround plans and see what impact they would have on
your profitability.

Building Your P&L Forecast

The easiest way to get started is to take a copy of last month's P&L and update it with the current month's revenue and any changes in expenses. Remember to use percentages so you can accurately predict cost of goods sold or other expenses that change based on sales volume.

Your first P&L forecast should analyze what it will look like if there are no changes in expenses or margins. Once you have this baseline P&L forecast, you can create different turnaround scenarios. What does it look like if you reduce expenses by 25%? Cut labor by 30%? Focus on higher margin products or reduce your cost of goods by 20%? What if you implemented all these ideas?

What if your percentages got back to where they were before your downturn? Build out this forecasted P&L with lower revenue levels.

Playing out different turnaround ideas with your P&L forecast is an important step in fixing your company. Seeing is believing and if you can get your P&L to show a profit, then you will know what areas need to change.

For example, based on the figures below, what would your forecasted P&L look like if you were able to cut labor by $15,000? Before you say, "that's impossible," just focus on the numbers, not how you will achieve the cuts. By focusing on the "what," not the "how," you can disconnect from much anguish and play around with the numbers until you find some potential turnaround strategies.

In Table 12-01 on page 114, we reduce the labor expenses by $15,000.

From this table, we see that cutting labor costs helped reduce your forecast losses. While it is a move in the right direction, it is not going to save the day. In most cases, it is not just one thing that you need to fix to get the company back to profitability (that would be too easy) but rather a combination of several ideas that will move you in the right direction.

Here is where your creative and visionary mind can have some fun. Your turnaround plan does not consist of just one P&L forecast. Instead, you will probably have ten or more, each running different scenarios and ideas that you have not yet committed to doing.

Maybe you wonder what your turnaround plan will look like if you reduce your staff and started working virtually to save on overhead expenses such as rent. Perhaps you can improve the margins of your top-selling products. The scenarios and numbers are different for everyone, but as you brainstorm and come up with different ideas, run P&L projections forecasting what your company will look like going forward.

	The Good Ole' Days	%	Current Meltdown	%	Forecast #1	%
Gross Revenue	$500,000		$250,000		$250,000	
Cost of Goods Sold	-$225,000	45%	-$175,000	70%	-$175,000	70%
Marketing & Sales	-$50,000	10%	-$40,000	16%	-$40,000	16%
Labor	-$50,000	10%	-$40,000	16%	-$25,000	10%
Operating Expenses	-$40,000	8%	-$40,000	16%	-$40,000	16%
Net Profit	$135,000		-$45,000		-$30,000	

Table 12-01

	The Good Ole' Days	%	Current Meltdown	%	Forecast #2	%
Gross Revenue	$500,000		$250,000		$250,000	
Cost of Goods Sold	-$225,000	45%	-$175,000	70%	-$160,000	64%
Marketing & Sales	-$50,000	10%	-$40,000	16%	-$25,000	10%
Labor	-$50,000	10%	-$40,000	16%	$25,000	10%
Operating Expenses	-$40,000	8%	-$40,000	16%	-$40,000	16%
Net Profit	$135,000		-$45,000		$0	

Table 12-02

Table 12-02 on page 115 is an example of changing multiple things within a company to achieve success. Notice how revenue was not one of the changes. This makes the chances of your success grow since cutting expenses is usually more within your control than your ability to increase sales.

Building as many different scenarios as you can come up with will clarify which turnaround ideas you should implement, and which ones you should not. Keep doing future P&L forecasting and goal setting until you get a P&L forecast that breaks even or shows a profit. Always asking yourself if your forecasts are conservative and realistic. If it is, there you go. You have your turnaround plan.

Once you have a turnaround forecasted P&L (or several) that look good, now comes the job of unpacking the simplified P&L so you can see the details within each category and find which specific costs you will eliminate or reduce.

The Compound Effect of Percentages

Creating a turnaround plan can be a daunting task, especially when you need to significantly slash your expenses by more than you think is possible. Cutting one area of your simplified P&L by 50%, for example, may not be possible. Fortunately, you do not just have one tool in your toolbox, you have several that can be used and could potentially add up to a significant change.

Often these small changes add up to more than the sum. Here is some funky math for you to consider.

$$10\% \times 4 = 50\%$$

You can see this does not look right, but it is correct. By simply finding four areas that you can improve by 10%, you may realize a 50% benefit. This funky math is accomplished via the compounding effect and is powerful in a turnaround scenario. The cuts, or improvements, feed from each other and add up to something greater than their sums.

For example, suppose you want to increase your gross margin on a product by 50%. Your accountant may tell you the only way to do that is with a substantial price increase. But by taking advantage of the compound effect of percentages, you could run a forecast P&L where you:

- Reduce manufacturing costs by 10%.
- Raise prices by 10% (customers probably will not even notice).
- Find 10% savings in freight costs: Reduce incoming freight costs and slightly increase shipping costs to the customer.
- Reduce storage costs, fulfillment costs, or packaging by 10%.

There are probably other ideas that create small percentage gains. It is far less daunting to find smaller gains.

How Often Do I Do This?

Mastering your financials is not a one and done proposition. It will take some time to understand your historical P&L and forecast a turnaround plan for your company. Your financials are fluid during a downturn, and so I suggest you monitor them daily.

Over time you will become more accurate with your forecasting ability, but it does take time. Do not look at this as a task you only work on during a downturn. Even when the turnaround is complete and you are profitable again, schedule two to three hours a month to dive deep into the prior month's numbers and adjust your forecast.

A great deal of this chapter has focused on the critical role of financial analysis in creating your turnaround plan. Financials are so crucial that I will be diving even deeper into the two main components of the P&L: revenue and expenses over the next two sections of this book.

Chapter 12: Action Steps

➢ Start forecasting the current month. Use last month's finalized P&L and update it with new revenue and expenses.

➢ Now start playing with different turnaround scenarios. What happens when you reduce certain expenses, improve margins, etc. Find a few turnaround plans that might get you to profitability.

SECTION THREE
OPTIMIZING YOUR
REVENUE

Not all revenue is created equal. ~Byron

That quote sounds so simple; you may be tempted to dismiss it. Do not! This section could be the most important one you will read if your company is struggling.

Not all revenue is equal. Period.

Revenue comes in a lot of different types and sizes. Some types of revenue are great and add meaningful contribution to your bottom-line. Other revenue may be profitable, but with only razor thin net profit margin. Some revenue is extremely complicated and difficult, resulting in high labor costs or high refunds.

When you are attempting to increase revenue, be sure you are focusing on the right type of revenue. Any increase in sales puts a strain on your company's systems and people. Do you want to strain those resources on low-profit revenue or high-profit revenue?

SECTION THREE: OPTIMIZING YOUR REVENUE

CHAPTER 13
SELLING MORE IS
NOT THE SOLUTION

If you stay in your comfort zone, you will become a prisoner of it. ~Berry Grimes

If your company started its downturn recently, my bet is that you initially thought the solution to the problem would be simply to increase sales. You are an entrepreneur. Growing sales is part of your DNA and you have been raised to believe that revenue fixes every problem, right? I understand and once thought that myself until I made a startling discovery. Unfortunately, that discovery came after receiving some really bad advice.

The Worst Advice I Ever Received

During Survival Frog's downturn, I hired a Chief Financial Officer (CFO) to consult with us on turnaround strategies.

He told me the solution to our decline was simply to increase sales volume. This came after thorough examination of our books and analyzing our current expenses. His advice was simply, "Just sell more."

The advice resonated with me, as I just wanted to get out of the mess. Increasing sales sounded easier than cutting costs and laying off employees.

We followed his guidance and focused on growing sales. Our efforts were successful and revenue went up, and I was excited to get our numbers at the end of the month. However, when I got the financial books back, it was like a punch in the gut. Even though our monthly revenue increased, we lost even more money!

I was devastated. How could that be?

Money coming in the door for one revenue source looks very much the same as money coming in for another. At first glance, even an "expert" CFO can assume all revenue is equal.

In a fit of desperation, I pulled an all-nighter digging into my P&L financials and pulled apart each of our revenue channels. What I discovered was astonishing.

I found that the particular revenue source we increased was not even profitable. In fact, for every $1 that Survival Frog brought in, we spent $1.15 to create it. The harder we worked, the more revenue we had, the more we would lose.

If I had done my homework first and not solely relied on an expert's advice, I could have saved our company significant time and expense. His advice to "just increase sales" was wildly misleading and could have led to the company's demise.

I fired that "expert" CFO the next day.

The advice I received was flawed on several layers. First is the general assumption that more revenue will fix the problem. In many cases, it just masks the core problem. Second, and most importantly, you cannot make such a general statement about sales revenue. Revenue comes in all shapes and sizes and is not created equally.

In the following chapters I will show you how to break down different types of revenue and decide which one to focus your precious time on.

When Cutting Revenue Makes Sense

I get it. The idea of reducing your revenue further sounds crazy. That is why you need to run the numbers and extrapolate a rough P&L for each of your revenue channels. That exercise will put a spotlight on which revenue source is helping you, and which is not.

Poorly performing revenue is hidden during the good times, so you do not see the damage done, but it is still there, stealing profit away from better-performing revenue. In essence, your best performing revenue is "funding" the losses of the bad revenue.

During growth times you may choose to invest in these losing revenue channels as a way of bringing in new customers. However, in a downturn, you simply cannot afford to have poorly performing revenue within your company. Only the most profitable revenue should be given your attention.

During Survival Frog's turnaround, we eliminated almost $1 million in revenue. On purpose! My team thought I had gone crazy. Even with the data supporting the decision it was a tough pill to swallow.

I assured my team we would consider bringing back this particular revenue source at a later time once we were profitable again. If you are struggling with the idea of cutting poorly performing revenue from your company, you may consider simply "pausing" the revenue for a period of time until you regain profitability. You may decide to never bring back that revenue, but that is a decision for the future.

In the next few chapters, I will show you how to determine the different revenue channels your business has, how to pull the data on each of those channels, and how to optimize it. And yes, that may result in you cutting or reducing a revenue channel.

Chapter 13: Action Steps

> ➤ Are you ready to take a hard look at each of your revenue channels? Which revenue does your gut tell you is your worst performing?

SECTION THREE: OPTIMIZING YOUR REVENUE

CHAPTER 14
TYPES OF REVENUE CHANNELS

Strength lies in differences, not in similarities.
~Stephen Covey

Before you can collect the financial data you will need, you must first understand the types of revenue your company produces. There are many different types of revenue channels, and most companies can do this exercise in various ways. The objective is to decide the best channels to focus your attention on.

Ask for help with this exercise from sales managers, accountants, and business associates. Make no mistake, however, that as the owner of the company, you are the one that needs to lead this project (where have you heard that before?).

In this chapter, I will introduce four ways to dissect your company's revenue sources, the objective being to find the best revenue channel to optimize, increase or even eliminate. The most common types of revenue channels are broken down by:

- Sales platforms
- Buyers
- Marketing
- Products

At first, this may be a difficult concept to grasp, and revenue channels will vary from company to company, so be prepared to review the information presented in this section more than once. Your mind may need a chance to digest the information, and a second or third run-through will give you more insight into this vital topic.

Remember, your goal here is to determine the best way to break apart your revenue channels so you can allocate various costs and determine profitability.

Types of Sales Platforms

A sales platform is how you sell your products or services. For example, your sales platforms may include retail product sales, wholesale product sales, or products sold online.

Your company will likely use more than one sales platform to generate revenue. Your goal is to analyze the revenue from each platform to find the winners and losers.

If your company only has one sales platform, you may not be able to analyze and optimize based on the sales platform.

For example, the owner of a residential cleaning company may have only one sales platform: cleaning services to the public. They are not selling retail products to customers, and their website generates no direct revenue. This company would not be able to divide up their revenue based on sales platforms.

Let's look at another example. Boats R Us is a company located in a resort marina. Over the years, they have created five specific revenue platforms: boat sales, boat rentals, a retail store in the marina, boat maintenance, and online merchandise sales. Each of those sales platforms can be analyzed and optimized for profitability.

If a large portion of your revenue comes from online sales, then that sales platform can be further broken down into sub-platform channels. For Survival Frog, we broke down our revenue platforms into E-commerce, Amazon sales, B2B wholesale and Direct Response Marketing. For any platform where you realize significant revenue, try and break it down further.

Types of Buyers

Another way to break down your revenue is by looking at the different types of buyers.

Two common types of buyers are B2B (business to business) and B2C (business to consumer). Selling to one of these buyer types is entirely different from selling to the other. For example, selling to consumers online is nothing like selling to corporate clients in person. The cost structure and related expenses are entirely different between these types of buyers. You want to dig into those numbers to analyze your net profits from each revenue channel.

When looking into buyer revenue sources, don't forget to consider marketing costs, commissions paid, employee salary, and all the other expenses in between.

Types of Marketing

If you have high marketing costs, you can break the revenue channels apart by the different marketing approaches used.

In today's cross-channel marketing world, it can be difficult to determine how much revenue comes from each of your marketing sources. Google Ads, Facebook, email, industry newsletters, trade shows and signage are examples of just a few marketing channels. A customer may see your advertisement on one or all these channels, and it is difficult to determine which brought in the sale.

However, there are ways to get close. Log into your paid marketing accounts and see your last 30-day results. Which one is doing the best for you? If it is still not clear, you may have a gut feeling of, dollar for dollar, what produces the best and worst results. Pick your marketing budget apart to see if there are clear winners or losers.

If search engine optimization (SEO) is a big focus for your company, you may believe that you do not have any marketing costs associated with it. Afterall, SEO is "free" organic traffic, right? Not really. Consider the direct labor or agency cost associated with optimizing your search engine results. Consider SEO as a marketing channel and analyze how much you spend versus your return on sales. If it is not profitable, consider pausing those efforts for a few months.

Once you find the problem areas in your paid marketing, focus on how you can optimize your marketing dollars. That could involve optimizing a campaign, reducing the size of a campaign, or even temporarily eliminating the marketing channel.

At Survival Frog, we found a way to reduce our marketing budget by 50%, while only decreasing sales by 10%. Read that last sentence again.

We knowingly reduced the revenue coming from marketing by 10%, but in exchange we cut our marketing budget of $100,000 in half. That had a big impact on our ability to quickly cut expenses. Most of that savings came from eliminating marketing in our poorly performing direct response platform.

There is an old marketing saying, "Half of my marketing is wasted; the trouble is I don't know which half." Now is the time to figure out what part of your marketing is not working and reduce it.

Types of Products (or Services)

Do you have specific products or services that are more profitable than others? Of course, you do. Do you know which are your top-performing products or services?

You can dig in and look at the specific data as it relates to product types. When analyzing types of products be sure to include all costs associated with the sale. Maybe one product has terrific gross margins, but when you add marketing costs and overhead, it makes little or no profit.

Another way of examining product data is to group products and services by category. At Survival Frog, some of our product categories are survival gear, food & water, energy & radio, kits, and camping. Each of these categories has its own attributes: margins, inventory cost, sell through rates, shipping costs, refunds and customer support levels.

In the next chapter, you will learn what types of revenue channels your specific business should examine closer.

Chapter 14: Action Steps

➢ Brainstorm and list out several ideas on how you can divide up your revenue channels based on the suggestions in this chapter.

SECTION THREE: OPTIMIZING YOUR REVENUE

CHAPTER 15
CHOOSING THE RIGHT
REVENUE CHANNEL

Torture the data, and it will confess to anything.
~Ronald Coase

Now that you have a good idea of what is meant by revenue channels, it is time to start looking at your numbers and making some decisions.

Everyone's business is different. What is right for my company may not be right for your business. You may not find a revenue channel that is actively losing money as Survival Frog did. Most companies in a downturn, however, will find *something* unexpected.

If all this talk about platforms, marketing, buyers, and products is confusing, I suggest you not focus on the details. Step back and look at your business with fresh eyes and ask the simple question: how does your company earn money? Does all your revenue come from one source, or do you have multiple revenue channels? How are the revenue channels different? How many ways can you classify revenue and produce a cost analysis for each?

Consider, as well, that your revenue channels could be a combination of one or more of the examples mentioned here. Breaking it down is not an exact science, and rough numbers are acceptable. After reading this chapter, however, you should have some ideas regarding your company's primary revenue channels.

Your ultimate goal is to divide your revenue into separate channels so you can decide which channels to optimize and which you should consider reducing or eliminating.

There are several ways of dividing up your revenue. It is less about getting it perfectly right and more about finding answers within the data.

Examples of Breaking Down Revenue Channels

Your goal is to find the biggest swing in performance between your revenue sources. How can you divide up your revenue and see the biggest winners and losers? Pick apart the poor performing revenue and find ways of optimizing for higher profits.

Joe's home remodeling example:

Joe owns a luxury home remodeling business, which does very little marketing. Most of Joe's customers are homeowners, and not commercial or industrial customers.

The type of services Joe offers, however, varies significantly. Therefore, Joe should begin his analysis by digging into the figures related to the different types of services (products) he offers.

He should create a P&L revenue breakdown for the three services he offers and their corresponding cost structure. That scrutiny will give Joe insight into which service he offers is his breadwinner and which might be hurting his company.

In the hypothetical, rough P&L breakdown on Table 15-01 on page 138, you can see that Joe has some useful data to comb through. His company is losing money, and if he increased sales across the board, he would most likely lose even more money.

However, if he were to increase the home office remodeling revenue and decrease or change the cost structure of his Deck/Porch revenue, he would be on his way to a turnaround.

	Basements	%	Deck/Porch	%	Home Office	%
Gross Revenue	$100,000		$200,000		$50,000	
Material	-$30,000	30%	-$80,000	40%	-$10,000	20%
Marketing	-$5,000	5%	-$15,000	8%	-$1,000	2%
Labor	-$50,000	50%	-$120,000	60%	-$15,000	30%
Sales & Commissions	-$10,000	10%	-$20,000	10%	-$5,000	10%
Profit	$5,000	5%	-$35,000	-18%	$19,000	38%

Table 15-01

Survival Frog example:

At Survival Frog, we found big performance swings in the platform (how we sold our products) combined with marketing expenses. We discovered that our Direct Response revenue channel was losing significant money. After unpacking that revenue, we found that it had high costs in marketing, software, and labor.

After breaking-down the revenue channels, we could see the performance varied from one source to the other.

The gross profits at the bottom of Table 15-02 on page 140 are not net profits. There are overhead costs that are not attributed to the revenue channels.

From this data, it was clear that the Direct Response revenue was a big issue for the company. This revenue came from online sales using long form HTML pages which were very tech labor intensive to create and manage. Once we added in the software used with this revenue source and the high marketing costs, it became clear to us that something had to change.

We made the difficult decision to restructure the Direct Response revenue channel and reduce 90% of the revenue. By doing so, we saw a drop in revenue of over $1 million a year. Gulp.

Our new lower revenue total, however, suddenly had much higher profit margins. What was left was a simple, ultra-efficient, and profitable revenue channel.

	e-Commerce	%	Amazon	%	B2B	%	Direct Response	%
Gross Revenue	$300,000		$50,000		$50,000		$100,000	
COGS (product cost)	-$150,000	50%	-$15,000	30%	-$30,000	60%	-$30,000	30%
Marketing Fees Affiliate	-$50,000	17%	-$15,000	30%	$0	0%	-$50,000	50%
Software	-$5,000	2%	$0	0%	$0	0%	-$15,000	15%
Direct Labor	-$10,000	3%	-$1,000	2%	-$1,000	2%	-$20,000	20%
Profit	$85,000	28%	$19,000	38%	$19,000	38%	-$15,000	-15%

Table 15-02

Survival Frog did not stop at just fixing one revenue channel, we also optimized e-commerce by lowering the product costs significantly, resulting in a higher profit margin. Amazon and B2B were profitable, so we put our efforts into growing those revenue channels.

When looking for your own broken revenue channels, look for areas with high product costs, expensive marketing, commissions, or runaway labor costs.

Size Does Matter

Even in good times, your company has limited resources and time to devote to various projects or revenue sources. During bad times, however, your ability to invest time and energy is limited even further. You are forced to be very selective in where you put your energy.

For this reason, you should consider the size of a particular revenue source before your company puts too much time into growing it. The size, or potential size, of a revenue channel must be considered before jumping into optimizing or growing it.

	Revenue A	Revenue B	Revenue C	Revenue D
Revenue	$150,000	$100,000	$25,000	$5,000
Profit	-$22,500	$20,000	$7,500	$2,000
	-15%	20%	30%	40%

Table 15-03

After reviewing the revenue sources listed on Table 15-03 on page 142, where do you think you should focus your attention when trying to increase sales? You may notice the high-profit margins in Revenue D. However, it has the lowest revenue levels and most likely will require the most effort to increase. To increase revenue by $5,000, Revenue B only needs a 5% increase, compared to a 100% increase in Revenue D to achieve the same dollar amount. Increasing Revenue B, or possibly C will give you a much better return on your effort.

Chapter 15: Action Steps

➢ Which method of breaking apart your revenue channels is the best for your company? List out a few different ways of dividing up your revenue. Then pick the one that makes the most sense to use first (you can do these exercises as often as you want using different scenarios).

SECTION THREE: OPTIMIZING YOUR REVENUE

CHAPTER 16
COLLECTING AND
ANALYZING THE DATA

*It is always wise to look ahead, but difficult to look
further than you can see. ~Winston Churchill*

Once you understand which revenue channels need further
investigation, it is time to collect the data you need. By
digging into the numbers on several different revenue
sources, you will start to see which channels have the best
and worst performance.

Collecting the Data

For each revenue channel, make a list of all expenses related to it. If you are uncertain whether to include a cost or not, consider this question:

"If I eliminate this revenue source, is it possible to also remove the related expense?"

That is a useful litmus test whether an expense ties to a particular revenue channel. Don't worry; you are not going to be cutting any revenue channels yet. But asking the question will help you decide if you should add the expense to the revenue channel's P&L.

General overhead expenses can be difficult to attribute to one specific revenue channel, but if you removed the revenue source, would you be able to eliminate 80% of the overhead expense? For example, one of your revenue sources may be a retail store, and without that revenue from retail sales, you would not need to pay rent. In this example add the rent expense to the retail revenue source.

In some cases, you may need to split up large expenses and attribute them to multiple revenue sources. You want to assign nearly every expense to one of the revenue channels, even if that means dividing things up.

Analyzing Revenue Channels

As we researched the data at Survival Frog, we discovered how much time and energy we wasted on a non-profitable revenue channel. Before the investigation, we had no idea that the revenue channel was full of problems. When we cut it, everything seemed to simplify itself, and we could move our time and focus to the other, more profitable revenue sources.

As I went through this examination for Survival Frog's revenue and helped other business owners do the same, I have found some best practices that will help you make this analysis most effective. Refer to Table 16-01 on page 148 as you read through these best practices.

Create a spreadsheet with percentages that shows a rough, simplified P&L per revenue channel, with all channels listed next to each other. It is critical that you include percentages next to the dollar amounts in your P&L spreadsheet, by dividing each expense line item by total revenue.

Without the percentages, Table 16-01 would be much harder to read. The $40,000 COGS in Revenue B is a tough comparison to the $10,000 COGS found within Revenue C until you can see that they both have the same 40% ratios. With percentages, you can associate varying dollar amounts in a fair comparison.

Focus on the big revenue that will make the most impact on your bottom line. Increasing revenue by 10% on a larger revenue channel will have a bigger impact than working on smaller revenue sources. As mentioned before, size does matter.

	Revenue Channel A		Revenue Channel B		Revenue Channel C		Revenue Channel D	
Revenue	$150,000		$100,000		$25,000		$5,000	
COGS	-$75,000	50%	-$40,000	40%	-$10,000	40%	-$1,500	30%
Marketing	-$60,000	40%	-$30,000	30%	-$5,000	20%	$0	0%
Other Costs	-$37,500	25%	-$10,000	10%	-$2,500	10%	-$1,500	30%
Profit	-$22,500	-15%	$20,000	20%	$7,500	30%	$2,000	40%

Table 16-01

Consider how you can lower expenses relating to a revenue source. Do not only look for ways to increase the revenue; you must also put thought into where you can cut costs associated with that revenue without hurting the profit margin. In some cases, this may result in the gross sales amount going down, but if your profit margin is better, you may find that you can bring the same amount of profit in the door.

Give extra attention to revenue sources with high growth potential. Realize that growing a revenue source places significant strain on your company's systems and demand on your employee's time, so make sure your efforts will pay off with more considerable growth potential. If a revenue source has the potential to grow 50% or more in the next few months and it has strong profit margins, then it warrants more effort from your team.

Take written notes as you do your research. Do not just try to think your way through this analysis. There is something about recording the data in spreadsheets and documenting your observations in your turnaround journal that will help you see the big picture and start connecting the dots.

Do not strive for perfection as you start to break down the different revenue channels. Remember that rough numbers are acceptable and even if your data were only 80% accurate, you would still be getting valuable insight into what has caused your downturn. There are multiple ways to break up your revenue channels, so don't think there is just one way to accomplish this analysis. Start somewhere and see where the data leads you.

Armed with the findings from your research, you are now ready to optimize your best revenue channels.

Chapter 16: Action Steps

- ➤ Divide up as many expenses as you can into your different revenue sources.
- ➤ Now analyze the data and determine your healthy and unhealthy revenue sources.

CHAPTER 17
OPTIMIZING REVENUE
CHANNELS

First optimize your revenue, then increase it. ~Byron

Your objective now is to optimize the revenue channels and turn your company into a profit producing machine.

What does it mean to optimize revenue? There are many scholarly definitions available that are hard to read and even harder to practice. My explanation of revenue optimization is much simpler:

Optimize Revenue: Increasing net profit by improving margins, reducing expenses, and finding efficiencies.

Notice that this definition does not mention anything about increasing revenue.

Optimizing revenue typically involves making your revenue channels more profitable. The gross revenue amount may actually decrease to achieve the goal of higher margins and efficiencies.

Most entrepreneurs' instinctive nature is to just work on increasing top line revenue. "I'm losing money, so I need to sell more" is the knee jerk reflex to a downturn.

I am not saying you should not increase revenue. What I am suggesting is you first optimize the revenue to maximize its profitability, and then you can increase the sales. Optimize first, increase second.

Optimize Good Revenue

Often the best way to optimize revenue is to start with your current winners. A tweak here and there to your healthy revenue channels can make a considerable contribution to your bottom line. Here are a few ideas.

- Can you ask your wholesale vendor to cut the cost of the product? If your company does not make it through the downturn, they will lose out as well. They may be very willing to work with you, even if it is a temporary reduction of cost.
- Does your product or service need all its features? Could you increase margins by eliminating some of the features that customers potentially do not use?

- Are you 100% sure you need the employees that are attached to this revenue? Could you do it with fewer employees, or would a contractor or agency be more economical?
- Could you reduce the commission percentage on this revenue source, even if it is just temporary?
- Could you simplify the packaging or shipping costs related to the revenue source?
- Is there a less expensive software option, or could you eliminate the software? Or could new software automate tasks and reduce labor costs?
- Can you lower the marketing cost to improve profitability as a percentage (reduce inefficient marketing by 50%, but only reduce sales 10%)?
- Can you charge more for shipping or installation of the product?
- Can you increase the price of the products?

A note about raising prices during a downturn: the concept may seem crazy at first, but do not dismiss it. Some of the best turnaround stories include raising pricing during the darkest of days.

Every industry is different, but you can often increase your prices by 5% or 10%, and your customers will not even notice. It is common (or at least it should be) for a company to raise prices every year to keep up with the cost of inflation.

When is the last time you increased your rates? Survival Frog raised its prices during our downturn 10%-20% on the top-selling products and had almost no pushback from customers.

Business to business accounts will require a conversation explaining why you are raising prices. With the right talking points, you'll get through any difficult meetings. Raising prices is a powerful way to increase margins, so give this serious consideration.

Most likely, none of the above measures alone will save your company, but a fantastic thing happens when you start making several small changes. Modest changes here and there begin to compound, and you begin to see significant change.

Optimize Marketing

I have mentioned this before, but it is vital to examine your marketing budget and see if there is room for optimization. At all times, and particularly during your turnaround, marketing is an area you need to be sure you are as efficient as possible.

During your downturn, it is less about cutting the dollars spent on marketing, and more about re-distributing your marketing resources to the areas that will make the most impact—in other words, optimizing your marketing spend.

In any marketing campaign, there is a core that is working exceptionally well. The larger the campaign's reach, the more customers you can find, but the less effective the marketing becomes.

During a downturn, you want to shrink the breadth of that marketing campaign to become more efficient. You may be able to narrow your marketing budget by 25–50% and only see a 5% or 10% decline in sales. Although you may reduce the marketing budget, the sales will not decrease by the same percentage; hence the margins improve.

To be clear, I do not recommend that you ever turn off your marketing completely. You need to continue marketing, even during a downturn. However, you may need to temporarily shift your mindset from offense to defense. Instead of growth, you may need to focus on where you can pull back and be more efficient?

There are likely hundreds of books with specific marketing techniques for your industry, so I will not cover every one of those techniques here. However, there are several areas where you may find efficiencies and the ability to lower costs within your marketing:

Reduce or eliminate branding and goodwill

Consider cutting branding and goodwill marketing completely during the downturn. That type of marketing is far away from the marketing efficiency core. You have no way of knowing the impact that type of marketing has on your bottom line. It may be essential when your company is in growth mode, but now, while you are trying to save the company, it can be put on pause.

Analyze quality spend with the 1/3 test

If forced to cut the bottom 1/3 of your marketing budget, where would you cut? You may not actually reduce the budget, but you will gain clarity by doing this exercise.

Rank your paid marketing sources and consider what is working and what is not.

If you cut the bottom 1/3 of the marketing budget, you might reduce the number of new customers slightly. Often, however, that bottom 1/3 of marketing is bringing in customers at a significant loss. That loss may be perfectly acceptable during your business's growth phases, but during a downturn, you need to adopt a different strategy.

You are in "cut the budget as deep as you can—so we can turn this ship around" mode. That bottom third of loss-leader marketing does not work during these difficult times.

Another option to consider as you do the bottom 1/3 exercise is whether you can reduce spending on individual campaigns without cutting them altogether. For example, you may spend $1,000 on Facebook ads and losing money. However, there is most likely $200 of that $1,000 that is very profitable at bringing in customers. Could you focus on that profit core and eliminate the worse performing $300?

The 80/20 Rule of Products and Services

The 80/20 rule states that 80% of revenue comes from 20% of the sales effort. Our goal as businesspeople is to develop the discipline to optimize and focus on the 20% that is beneficial and put less effort on the 80%, which is often far less efficient.

The 80/20 rule is particularly meaningful when it comes to determining what products to focus your sales efforts on.

During Survival Frog's turnaround, we drastically reduced our product offerings. Before the downturn, we had a reputation as having the best selection of survival products. We had the widest variety and took pride in offering every obscure product you could think of.

However, when we analyzed our product mix, we saw that many products were not profitable enough. By taking a hard look at the best 20% of our product selection we were able to find opportunities.

We ended up reducing our product offerings from 550 items to just 175. It was heartbreaking. I was sure that all our loyal customers would wonder where our extensive product line went and complain. I watched and waited for those complaints to pour in. Guess how many we received?

None.

We were able to remove 375 products from our website and remain relevant to our customers. That also significantly improved our average product margins and simplified the business. This one change had a significant impact on our ability to turnaround the company.

I recall a story I heard about a struggling company that hired a high-level consultant to help turn their business around. During a meeting with the executive team, the consultant asked the managers to gather a sampling of every product they sold and place them on the conference room table.

Although there were hundreds of products, they reluctantly complied. They piled hundreds of products on the conference table. It was overflowing.

Next, the consultant told the group to arrange the products in descending order, with the most popular at the head of the line, moving down to the least popular products at the end of the line. The executives were getting impatient, but they complied with the request. It took hours. When the consultant returned, the team was ready to rebel. "This better be good," they grumbled. Our business is in decline, and you are having us do this crazy exercise. We just need your advice on the turnaround."

The consultant went over to the conference table and estimated the top 20% of the products. With a big, bold swipe, he knocked the remaining 80% off the table. As hundreds of products crashed to the floor, the executives' mouths fell open in astonishment. What the heck was this guy doing?!

"Now," the consultant said to the speechless group. "This 20% is the only thing we are going to focus on until we save your company."

And that simple exercise turned the company around.

Examine your product or service mix. What makes up the top 20% of that merchandise or services? During your downturn, it is essential to focus almost exclusively on that top 20%. When your turnaround is complete, and things are good again, you can loosen up on this rule, but for now, dedicate all your resources to your top 20% of products or services.

When Survival Frog eliminated over 350 products, we were able to focus on the most profitable, highest sales volume products that remained. It simplified our business tremendously and we therefore increased our efficiency. The liquidation of those discontinued products also provided a much-needed cash injection to increase our cash runway.

Again, to my surprise, none of our customers complained about the reduced product selection. We monitored the situation closely, and I even personally called some of our high-volume customers. No complaints. No one noticed.

Your results could be different and you may find a few customers who are upset. But consider that even if you did receive a few complaints, it may be worth it. Would that be an acceptable outcome if it helped you reduce your product count and save your company a significant amount of money?

I realize now that even if we had received some complaints, it would have still been worth it.

Better to have a few upset people and stay in business than to have everyone happy right up to the day we went bankrupt. If that happened, how many disappointed customers would we have? All of them.

Here is the best part. Once we had narrowed our product mix down to just the highest profit-generating 175 products, the result was that we increased our overall gross margin by 50%. Boom!

For Survival Frog, the reduction in products was temporary and we only maintained that extreme curtailment for about six months. It worked wonders to bring us back from the brink of disaster. Today, we are adding new products, because we are profitable and in growth mode once again. The experience taught us a lot of valuable lessons, however, and we now add new products differently. We are smarter and calculate the expected profit margins and how it will impact cashflow and inventory.

There are several benefits to just focusing on the top 20% of products:

- You stock less inventory.
- You simplify your business.
- You focus more time and energy on marketing your best products and services.
- You bring in immediate cash by liquidating the products you are removing.

If you think it is impossible to cut any of your products, could you instead just "pause" some of them for a couple of months? What could happen if you focused all your time and energy on just the top 20% of your products?

Chapter 17: Action Steps

We have talked about possibly cutting or reducing bad revenue or poorly performing products and services, but now is the time to pull the trigger and make those decisions.

➢ Which revenue channels can you "optimize" by fixing, reducing, or eliminating?
➢ What are five things you can do to increase your margins and reduce expenses (including marketing costs) on your best performing revenue?
➢ How can you apply the 80/20 rule to your products or services? Put most of your effort into that 20% that produces 80% of the results.

SECTION THREE: OPTIMIZING YOUR REVENUE

CHAPTER 18
INCREASING REVENUE

There are only three ways to increase revenue. ~*Jay Abraham*

Once you have highly optimized, profitable revenue sources, it is time to increase sales. There are legitimately only three ways to increase your company's revenues:

1. Get more customers.

2. Get your customers to spend more on each purchase.

3. Get your customers to buy more often.

#1–Get More Customers

Let me say right up front that in a downturn, getting more customers is by far the hardest of the three strategies.

When you are working on getting more customers, there are two areas to focus on; the number of prospects or leads, and the conversion ratio in closing the sale. The formula looks like this:

Number of Prospects x Conversion Rate = Sales

100   X   20%   =   20 Sales

There are two factors in the above formula that you can influence. If you increase either one, your sales will increase. Of course, you should eventually work to improve both!

Increasing the number of prospects

Sales leads are defined differently by every business. For the sake of this book, let us consider leads to include:

- the number of people who see your website
- the number of inbound or outbound phone calls your company handles, or
- the number of people walking into a retail store.

Raising your conversion rate

Once you have figured out how to increase your leads with marketing efforts, you need to focus on improving your conversion rate. How can you increase your ratio of successfully creating a new sale?

Raising your conversion rate is often less expensive than attracting more prospects, and you are trying to conserve cash during a downturn so this is a great area to focus your attention during a turnaround.

Most likely, you already know what increases your chances of making the sale: better salesmanship, building better relationships and having engaging website pages that convert leads to customers.

#2–Get Them to Spend More on Each Purchase

Another way to increase revenue is to have your customers spend more money with you whenever they purchase. Getting a customer who is already going to buy from you to spend 10-20% more on their current purchase is relatively easy. Increasing AOV (average order value) can be a windfall of profits for most companies.

"Do you want fries with that?" This phrase was made famous among marketers by McDonald's because that one single sentence made millions of dollars for the company.

There are many ways to offer an upsell or add-on. For online sales, it can be done both before the purchase and after the sale with software apps.

On the phone, you can wait until the customer agrees to buy the product and has given you payment details, then simply offer, "For just $___ more, I can add on XYZ product or service. Should I go ahead and add that to your order?"

Once you have your customer ready to buy, that is the time to offer them more. Psychologically, they have already gotten over the barriers and made their big decision to buy from your company. Their trust is higher, and they are somewhat euphoric, quite possibly open to other products or services. Now is the best time to ask for the additional sale.

What add-ons, up-sells, or complementary products can you offer your customers to increase their final purchase price? You could provide faster shipping options, product insurance, pre-paid service support, a one-hour consultation, and more. The ideas are limitless. Figure out what your ideal customer wants and then offer it to them.

#3–Inspiring Customers to Buy More Often

Getting a customer to buy again is much easier than going out to find a new customer. Yet so few companies make repeat customer marketing a priority.

When an existing customer purchases something from you again, you do not have the same marketing costs as with a new customer, so these buyers are much more profitable. They have more trust in your company and will typically spend more with you.

Consider a few of these ideas to increase sales from repeat buyers:

- A coupon for a percentage off the second purchase.
- A free item when they come back and buy again (often this is cheaper than discounting).
- "Retargeting" ads for things they considered but did not buy.
- Send a piece of direct mail to remind them of an event or a sale.
- Pick up the phone and call your previous VIP buyers.

What if you only have one product or just a few offerings? I would suggest finding new or complementary products that you can offer to those customers. They do not even have to be your products. You could find a few affiliate offers and get paid a commission when they buy. There are countless ways to monetize your current customers.

In Summary...

At this point, you can see that the first option, getting more customers, is the most challenging task. Most people start with this when seeking to increase their sales revenue and give up when it does not work quickly enough.

Remember that there are only three ways to increase sales. Despite what appears to be thousands of options out there, it really comes down to the three strategies we just covered. Brainstorm a list of 5 ideas within each strategy, then start testing your ideas.

Chapter 18: Action Steps

- ➢ List 5 potential ways to get more customers.
- ➢ List 5 potential ways to get your customers to spend more on each purchase.
- ➢ List 5 potential ways to get your customers to buy more often.

SECTION FOUR
CUTTING EXPENSES
AND FINDING
EFFICIENCIES

Your company needs you to make some big, bold decisions. Rock the boat, shake things up and let everyone know you are executing your turnaround plan. ~Byron

We have already discussed getting your financials in order in Section 2 and optimizing your revenue channels in Section 3. We touched a little on cutting expenses related to your revenue streams to make them more profitable.

In this section, we are going to dive deeply into the concept of cutting expenses.

Do *not* put this book down! I know what you are thinking.

Admittedly, cutting expenses is an entrepreneur's least favorite activity. Probably the only thing worse than cutting overhead and expenses is letting employees go. We will save that topic for Section 5 of the book.

Are we having fun yet?

It is essential that you do not brush past this section, or think you have already cut some costs, so you don't need to focus on this area anymore. I personally had several "Okay; I'm done, I've cut expenses," moments. I have thought more than once, "We've already cut so deep, there aren't any more expenses we can cut."

Whatever *your story* is, this section will give you strategies that you can use to cut expenses in a healthy way for the company, for your team, and yes, for your sanity.

The *story* I was telling myself about certain expenses and pet projects within Survival Frog was one of denial. Before our downturn and even into the first three months, I was in denial about our expenses.

I honestly thought Survival Frog was efficient and not wasting any money on non-essential expenses. How wrong I was!

Sure, I knew we had a few costs we could cut, but did not think they would add up to much. I believed we needed most of those extra expenses to run the business. I justified a lot of waste because we were previously growing, and any excess was a result of our growth. All that had to change now that we were in a downturn.

Maybe you, too, believe you have already cut all extra expenses and run a highly efficient company. However, if you stick with me and work thoughtfully through this section, I predict you will look back in a few months and be shocked at how much further you were able to cut.

You might not be excited about cutting costs. I get that.

You may not be excited about laying people off. I *really* get that.

Are you excited about getting back to profitability? Do you want a company that survives this downturn and comes out the other side far more efficient?

That is what this section can do for your company. Cutting expenses is a requirement for your turnaround to be successful. You cannot skip this step.

SECTION FOUR: CUTTING EXPENSES
AND FINDING EFFICIENCIES

CHAPTER 19
THE FASTEST WAY TO PROFIT

Dollar for dollar, cutting expenses is the fastest way to profitability. ~Tim Francis

You may think that the fastest way to profitability is to increase sales. If you can find a way to increase sales, go for it! But do not rely on that strategy alone to save the day.

What if you cannot double sales? Or what if you can, but not fast enough to build a cash runway that will protect your company?

If increasing sales is your only plan, then you are in trouble.

Don't get me wrong. The best possible scenario would be one where you can increase your revenue <u>and</u> cut your expenses. Sales alone will rarely rescue your company.

If doubling sales does end up saving your company, it is just a Band-Aid fix. You will be picking this book back up again in 6–12 months to deal with the core problems.

Cutting Expenses is the Fastest Way to Profitability

Cutting expenses is absolutely the *fastest* way to get back to profitability. Dollar for dollar it is even faster than increasing revenue. I know it sounds bizarre, but consider the return on investment (ROI) of both scenarios, as demonstrated on Table 19-01 on page 175.

The oversimplified table demonstrates that when you increase revenue by $1,000, you are not adding $1,000 to the bottom line. There are expenses related to that sale that reduce the impact. For this example, I used only COGS related to the product, but in reality, there would be several other expenses (e.g., marketing, commissions, labor). In this very conservative example, $1,000 additional in sales only increased net profit by $500. In reality the profit may only be a few hundred dollars.

However, as you can see in the table, cutting costs produced a $1:$1 value. The $1,000 in reduced expenses contributed $1,000 right to the bottom line. The concept is a game-changer. Look at the table again. I want you to genuinely understand that the fastest and most effective way to fix your company's profitability is, hands down, to cut your expenses, and do it as quickly as you can.

	Original		$1,000 Increase in Sales		$1,000 Decrease in Expenses	
Sales	$10,000		$11,000		$10,000	
COGS (50%)	-$5,000	50%	-$5,500	50%	-$5,000	50%
Expenses & Overhead	-$3,000	30%	-$3,000	27%	-$2,000	20%
Net Profit	$2,000		$2,500		$3,000	
Benefit (ROI on $1,000)			$500	50%	$1,000	100%

Table 19-01

Another good thing about cutting costs is that it has predictable outcomes. Increasing revenue is anything but predictable in a down market, so working on activities where you can predict the result is a smart move.

Cutting Fast

You may be saying, "Byron, you're right. I need to cut costs. I am going to think all of this through and probably start cutting next month."

Curtailing expenses is easy to procrastinate. You are an entrepreneur, and you are wired for growth, not retreating. I urge you to resist that temptation to procrastinate.

Your ability to not just cut expenses, but to do it quickly can make the difference between surviving, or not.

If your current cash runway is three months, meaning you will be out of cash in three months, what does a reduction in expenses look like? If you were to cut $10,000 in expenses, would your cash runway be extended to three and a half or even four months? Do the math by working some significant expense cuts into your P&L forecasting to see the effect.

The longer you wait to cut an expense, the more damage you cause to your cash runway and your ability to turn your company around. You are not just prolonging the issue, you are cutting directly into your company's survivability. Tick-tock, tick-tock.

Another reason you immediately need to start cutting expenses is that there is often a delay in seeing the benefits. Once you pull the trigger on a decision to cut a cost, the expense does not always stop immediately. You may be on a 30-day billing cycle, or you may have contracts in place that prevent you from cutting the cost instantly. You may have to wait 30 days or 90 days or six months. Decide now. Cancel today! The faster you do it, the quicker you will see the results.

Making it a Provisional Cut

Your company is in trouble. You know you must cut (and deep) to save it, but it hurts. It hurts to cut software that makes the job easier or shut down a pet project that is not making money yet.

Stop thinking of the cuts as forever. Instead, could you simply "pause" the expense? Once you execute your turnaround plan, you can always add back the expenses later.

Pausing is a strategy we used particularly well at Survival Frog. We had a lot of software that we "needed," although after looking at it further, we agreed we could *pause* the use of it for a few months. We rationalized that we could do anything for a few months, so everyone agreed to pause the expense to see how things would work without it.

To our surprise, we didn't really need a lot of those things, and as you probably guessed, we didn't bring back the extra expenses even when we could afford it later.

Can you cut the expenses for six months or a year to save your company? It may not be easy, but you can deal with it. This turnaround phase is only temporary; you can always go back to your old ways later.

You can restart those pet projects and try and rehire the employees later. At this point, you are defending your company and drastic changes are needed.

My prediction is that you will look back a few years from now and be shocked at how inefficient and wasteful your company had become before the downturn. I doubt you will add back in most of the costs you cut even when you can afford them.

Chapter 19: Action Steps

> ➢ What *story* are you telling yourself when it comes to cutting expenses? How will those decisions affect your cash runway? Write your thoughts in your journal.

CHAPTER 20
FINDING WHERE TO CUT

Never let a good crisis go to waste. ~Winston Churchill

Your business is different from any other, so the costs and expenses you need to cut are unique. Nevertheless, some major categories are similar across most companies. In this chapter, we discuss where you will find the most considerable cost savings and the most common areas of waste within a company.

Labor

Labor is likely the most significant expense on your P&L statement, making it the biggest lever you must manage. I know the thought of cutting labor makes you apprehensive and nervous. You no doubt dread the day when you will have to lay off employees.

Because labor is so crucial to your company's success, I dedicated Section 5 of this book to managing your human resources, including how to cut those resources when you must.

Software

Software costs seem to creep up over time. Software includes subscription costs for all those programs and tools you use to make life easier for you and your employees, including data analysis, project management, workspace organization, video conferencing, and other collaboration tools. They are easy to justify at the time since anything that makes our lives easier is allowed. After all, it is only $59 a month, right? However, those monthly recurring charges can add up to big bucks over time.

In Chapter 21, I will be introducing my color-coded method for determining which costs you should cut and when. This strategy is especially useful for software because it disciplines you to identify every software tool you pay for regularly, what you use it for, and how critical it is for your business. You will find the company can live without many software programs, either on an interim basis or permanently. You may even find some software expenses you didn't realize you had.

Office

The days where you need a traditional office to conduct business are gone. For many business owners, this is a tough area to consider cutting (or pausing). Survival Frog had a 12,000 square foot office and warehouse where our 27 employees worked.

I loved the office, and I had a lot of pride and emotional attachment to the idea of having an office. I also had three more years on my lease term, so a lot was keeping me there.

Every situation and every company is different, so I am not saying everyone should shut down their offices and go virtual. I am sure your list of reasons to keep your office is longer than the list of reasons to shut it down. It is normal to have those feelings, but it is crucial to step away from any legacy business concepts and rethink what is required to run your business.

Is it possible to go without an office for a few years as you rebuild the company? Could you get out of your lease, or even sublet the building? If you own your building, does it make sense to sell? Could you reduce the portion of your office that you use and sublet the rest?

Once Survival Frog shut down the office, moved the warehouse to an outsourced fulfillment center, and found a tenant, we saw enormous savings. There was an additional wave of expenses that also disappeared, including utilities, common area adjustments, maintenance, improvements, cleaning, and trash removal. We found dozens of smaller hidden costs, such as bottled water, office supplies, and furniture. It all adds up and going virtual helped reduce our losses and set us up for future success.

Shutting down the Survival Frog office was a "pause" expense. I am planning on having an office in the future. Nevertheless, owning and operating a virtual company has made it healthier in many ways and has been a great experience.

I challenge you to ask yourself: *What would it look like for your business to go virtual or partially virtual?* Mapping out what it might look like does not commit you, so grab a pen and paper and plan what you would do if you had to go virtual to save the business.

You may need to borrow or hire a conference room or find another location for manager and client meetings. You may have to utilize Zoom or Skype for your weekly team meetings. Nevertheless, there are solutions. To my surprise, our company culture is stronger than ever since we started working virtually. Push yourself on this. Is there any possible way to get rid of the office during the turnaround?

Allow me to expand a bit on the topic of employee engagement. A common fear when considering going virtual is that your employees will not be as committed to giving 100% to their work. Let me ask you this: Even if an employee is only 80% as productive working from home if you did the math, would an employee working at 80% still save more money than getting 100% but spending massive overhead on the office? I believe the answer is yes.

It is true that some people just cannot work well from home. Remote working will not be a good fit for everyone, and you may need to part ways. Nevertheless, I found that hiring top-quality employees got much easier when we advertised that we do 90% of the work remotely. It opened a massive pool of candidates that are efficient and qualified to work from home.

Our efficiency improved as well. Remote working does not encourage idle chit chat all day long that pulls a person away from their work both physically and mentally.

Warehouse or Fulfillment Centers

At Survival Frog, we not only went virtual with the office and employees, but we also outsourced our product fulfillment. I hated this idea because we did a fantastic job of fulfillment, and we had much pride in this area.

Moving to a Third-Party Logistics Center (3PL) was terrifying because I knew they would not do as great a job as we could in-house. And you know what? I was right. They do not do as good a job. In our situation, a 3PL did make more mistakes than we did.

However, when looking at the big picture the 3PL fulfillment center was probably 90% as good. And the savings we realized once we were able to shut down the warehouse were huge.

Sometimes there is an acceptable level of problems if the savings are large enough. Survival Frog had to allow for some inconveniences and a "less than perfect" scenario to fully realize the potential savings.

What is your one huge expense that you do not want to cut–the one thing that seems impossible? What is the thing that has a long list of reasons why you could never change?

Survival Frog is known for its high quality and amazing customer service. We are fanatics about it. Ultimately, however, we realized that despite the inevitable fallout from outsourcing our fulfillment, it was an acceptable loss, and we had to get over it.

Here is the thing: you may want to have the world's best customer support and live up to standards your company has set. You can strive to service 100% of your customers with 100% customer satisfaction, but if you are out of business, how many customers can you serve? 0%.

Who benefits? Your customers certainly don't. They are upset you went out of business, and now they must go to your competitor, and we all know they are not as good as you.

If you can live with the *almost* perfect customer experience in a downturn, there may be some big savings for your company. We did this with fulfillment, and to a lesser degree, with our support department as well. That was a tough mental dilemma for us to work through because of the high importance we place on happy customers. We even have a slogan "Amazing Buying Experience" that we had to live up to (our legacy standard).

We eventually found a 3PL that ended up shipping faster than we were previously able to do, and once we considered the savings in rent and labor, it was a considerable boost to the bottom line.

I want to emphasize this one more time–I hated the idea of shutting down the office and fulfillment center, but we did what we had to do. We stayed in business.

Marketing Spend

Marketing is not an area I recommend you cut costs too aggressively. One of the worst things you can do during a downturn is to reduce your pipeline of leads or traffic to your website. Nevertheless, it is essential to be smart with the marketing dollars you spend. As discussed in Chapter 17, cutting a portion of your marketing budget may not have a big impact on sales. Only the top one third of the money you spend on marketing during good times has excellent ROI, contributing to most of your sales. The other two-thirds of your marketing budget is less effective and is where you can find some savings.

Table 20-01 is an example of cutting the marketing budget in half while only having a minimal reduction in sales:

Marketing Budget	Spend	Number of Sales	Cost per Sale
Current	$10,000	100	$100
Cut Budget in Half	$5,000	80	$62

Table 20-01

Because of inefficiencies that nearly every marketing budget has, you can reduce your spending significantly while only reducing your sales slightly. If the math above was correct for your company, would it be worth saving $5,000 to forgo 20 sales? That is a question you should explore with your team.

Marketing agencies

Marketing contractors or agencies come with a cost, and it is an area you may want to consider cutting for the short term. General agency costs are about 15% of the marketing spend (Facebook, Google, etc.) per month.

	Current	Cut Agency	Cut Agency & Budget Inefficiencies
Revenue	$50,000	$50,000	$40,000
COGS (50%)	-$25,000	-$25,000	-$20,000
Marketing Spend	-$25,000	-$25,000	-$12,500
Agency Cost	-$3,750	-$0	-$0
Profit	**-$3,750**	**$0**	**$7,500**

Table 20-02

How do the numbers look after you cut agency costs? How about if you were also to reduce the inefficient marketing and branding you are currently paying for?

In some cases, you can run the marketing campaigns without the agency. You would not do advanced optimization or increase the campaigns; you would only log into the platform and check the data. If the numbers look good, you leave it alone. Of course, you will need to know what numbers to look for and how to make some basic adjustments along the way, which can be readily learned on YouTube or from a friend experienced in online marketing.

Not every company can, or should, fire their marketing agency and fly solo. I am just sharing my personal experience and have done it a few times before. Each time we have been able to manage through the transition and save some money.

For the record, I like using marketing agencies and continue to use them now. I get much value from their services, and they have helped us grow over the years. But there is a time and place for everything, and for my company, we were able to find savings here. You may, too. Once the market rebounds and you get back to profitability, then bring them back on to help grow your business.

Pet Projects

Pet projects are those favorite projects of yours that were started a while back. You know the ones that you expect could double your sales or revolutionize the industry, but the project has not yet brought about that result. When your company is in a downturn, these are the projects you need to pause for a time.

Pet projects can be a blind spot for many entrepreneurs, and you will find yourself justifying and even denying the amount a pet project is hurting the company during the downturn. You need to get over it and stop throwing good money after bad. There is a time and place for everything, and now is not the time to "invest in the future."

Any business activity that is not directly giving you profitable revenue now, needs to be paused. Even if it will cost you more money to restart it back up later, it should be put on hold during the downturn.

You cannot be working on projects that are going to change the world six months from now. You might be bankrupt in six months. You need to retreat and build your profitability and cash runway before you restart a pet project.

All the Little Stuff

Finally, you can cut significant dollars from your expenses merely by analyzing all the "little stuff." These are costs such as office supplies, meals, entertainment, and yes, even the bottled water in the office. These items add up to a lot, so do not dismiss them.

To be honest, I started off reducing expenses at Survival Frog quite modestly, but with each passing month, I became more and more disturbed by the losses. My cash runway was dwindling, and my chance for turnaround along with it.

One month, in a fit of despair, I cut everything down to the bare bones. We slashed anything that was not mandatory to conduct business. I only wish I had done that sooner.

A word of warning as you start cutting expenses in all the categories described in this chapter. You will find all kinds of skeletons in the closet—and ugly ones, including employee theft, complete disregard for common sense purchases, and software that you have maintained subscriptions for years without ever using. It can be humiliating. Do not beat yourself up, it is quite common.

Now that you have a better idea of what areas you need to make cuts, here is how to make it happen.

Chapter 20: Action Steps

> ➤ What areas of your company can you cut expenses? Don't worry about "how" to cut those expenses. Focus on the "what" to cut first.

CHAPTER 21
COST CUTTING STRATEGIES

Control your expenses better than your competition. This is where you can always find the competitive advantage. ~Sam Walton

I hope you are warming up to the fact that decreasing expenses wherever feasible is the fast track to turning your company around and renewing profitability. Knowing where to start, however, can be overwhelming. I delayed this process with Survival Frog longer than I should have.

In this chapter, I would like to share strategies to help make cutting costs a little easier. Remember, the sooner you decrease your expenses, the better chance you will have of saving your company.

Get Your Team Involved

In Section 5, we will discuss how to best communicate the downturn to your employees, but for now, let's just say you need to be honest with them. Let them know the business is in trouble, and their jobs could be at risk. If you have a good turnaround plan and get everyone involved in the solutions, the chances of employees quitting are greatly reduced.

Often, a business owner pretends everything is fine and carries the burden on his or her shoulders for as long as possible. But in a downturn, everyone must pitch in and make a sacrifice to turn things around. That means no expensive holiday dinners, no retreats, no bonuses, no raises, no new anything!

Depending on how bad things are, you most likely need to cut everything that is not critical infrastructure required to run the business (and then second guess everything you think is "critical").

Every $5 cut proves the point to your team that you are making changes that will help the company make its turnaround and save jobs. Your employees should see these cuts as positive momentum in executing the business turnaround.

Cut Deep, Make it Hurt

When cutting expenses, cut deeper than you think is required; you can always add the cost back later. If the process does not hurt, then you have not cut enough.

At the level where you feel comfortable cutting, go 20% or 30% deeper than that. That still may not be far enough. I cut what I thought was a lot of costs, and yet we still had to come back and cut more. And then more.

Don't be scared to rock the boat. In fact, I encourage you to rock the boat and rock it good. Your employees will not see the turnaround as the real deal if there are no significant changes.

Remember that once you have declared to your team and vendors that you are executing an aggressive turnaround plan – they expect big things.

Give them what they are expecting. Cut deep and do it quickly. Make big changes that rock the boat and disrupt the "normal ways" of doing things.

You Will Have a Different Company When Done

Some of the best advice I can give you is to accept the idea that this downturn will change your company. You cannot survive a significant downturn and come out looking the same. Your company is going to look different in many ways, and you may not initially like all the changes. However, I believe you will love the changes to the company when it's all done.

Your company will be more profitable and streamlined. It will be more efficient and will be a much more reliable company that can better handle any future downturns. It will probably even have a better culture than before. It will be a better company, but getting there, that is tough.

Watch for signs where you feel that you may be holding on to old ideas or legacy expenses. Rock the boat and get aggressive with cutting costs. Your company will look different when you are done.

Who Should Lead the Effort in Cost Cutting?

The task of slashing your company's expenses can just be handed off to your bookkeeper, right?

No.

So, who should oversee the expense reduction? The answer is you! As I have mentioned a few times before, you have the most to lose if your company fails, and you will do the best job at this vital task.

Delegating this to someone else will lead to problems as the rest of the team questions the individual in charge and their motivations. If the one leading the efforts is you, it will go over so much better.

You can recruit help, especially in the analysis of the financials and the actual implementation of cutting the costs. For the decision-making portion, and how you communicate it to the team, you need to be the one leading the efforts.

Another area that you, as the owner, should step in is in contacting vendors if you expect issues with canceling or breaking contracts. You will be able to negotiate a way out of your commitment better than any other employee. You may not need to call each vendor, but for the larger accounts it usually makes sense for the owner to make the call.

I suggest that throughout your turnaround, you approve every extra dollar that gets spent. Does that add more time to your already crazy workload? Yes, it certainly does. That diligence, however, is how you will fix the company. You can always delegate the task again later, once your company is back to profitability.

Color Coding Expenses

This strategy *really* helped me cut expenses. I implement this exercise when coaching clients, and it is always a useful tool. It is a simple strategy but will take some time to set up. You may want to enlist help to gather the data.

Begin by listing out all your expenses in one spreadsheet. The cashflow forecast exercise you did earlier will provide most of the data you need here. Include every single expense your company has seen over the last six months. Go into your accounting program, credit card statements, and bank account and pull anything you have paid in the past six months. Then note the frequency. Some charges may be one-offs, but many will be monthly, quarterly, or annually.

Once you have completed the spreadsheet, you will have several pages and hundreds of expenses listed out. You can categorize the expenses or just leave in a long list.

When you have a relatively comprehensive listing of your expenses, color code them green, yellow, or red, according to your ability to cut the cost. In this exercise, you need to color-code every single expense, regardless of how small it is.

Red–you could cut expenses immediately

Yellow–maybe you can cut, but no sure yet

Green–must keep, critical infrastructure

Red are the costs that you can cut right now. You may not want to do it; but when you look at the expense and ask yourself if you can live without it, you know you can. Label all the easy to cut expenses in red.

Next, move to green. Green are the mission-critical expenses that the business cannot do without. These expenses are part of your infrastructure. You literally cannot operate without them, or at least that is what you currently think.

Yellows are your "maybes." Maybe you can cut them; maybe you need them. Perhaps you need them now but will trim them later. If you are not yet sure, mark them yellow.

Once your list is color-coded, you have some action to take:

Start cutting the red expenses immediately. Make the phone calls. Cancel the subscriptions. Do whatever you need to do to get rid of the reds.

In his fantastic book, *Profit First: Transform Your Business from a Cash-Eating Monster to a Money-Making Machine,* Mike Michalowicz explains that one of the quickest ways to reduce your monthly credit card expenses is to cancel the card. Call the credit card company and tell them you lost your card and want a new number. They will send you a replacement, but all those auto-rebill charges you get every month will automatically be declined because you now have a new credit card number.

When the vendor tells you the payment did not go through, you can give them your new card number for those mission-critical greens, but do nothing for the red expenses you wanted to cancel. It is a quick way to stop those rebills and to get ahead of any future payments before being charged.

Organize the greens and yellows. After you cancel the red expenses, list out the greens and yellows in order of importance. Put the top mission-critical expenses at the top of the green section and continue down in order of importance. Do the same exercise for the yellow costs listing the expenses most likely to be cut later near the top of the list. Now you know where to go when you need to cut more costs in later phases of the turnaround.

Take another look at those yellow and green expenses. Can they be pushed to the red category, at least temporarily? Every time I went through this exercise (and I went through it about five rounds before my turnaround was complete), I found that what I thought was critical to the company was, in fact, a "nice to have." Removing it did not result in the doom of the company as I feared.

Look for waste in the green and yellow categories. At Survival Frog, we found that we had two software subscriptions for software that did relatively the same function. It often happens when you have had the software subscription for a while. When we started using one of the software programs, it only had one purpose. But over time, it was updated and improved to include the functions we were paying for in the other software. We had no idea. That allowed us to move the second software to red and cancel the subscription.

Find cheaper green and yellow options. Most likely, a lot has happened in the industry since you initially subscribed to a product or service. Maybe you only had one or two choices back in the day. Now over a dozen companies are offering the same thing, and rates may have gone down for the same product or service. Visit the vendor's website and see if there are any introductory prices you can negotiate into.

Just a reminder that these cuts can be provisional or temporary. Ask yourself if you could pause an expense and go without it for three months. After the three months, allow yourself to add it back in (if you think you still need it).

Remember, every dollar saved in expense is a dollar more in profit (or a dollar less in losses). The one to one ratio is amazingly powerful. Challenge yourself on those yellows and greens. How can you push them to red?

Renegotiating With Vendors

I have always been the type of person that pays his bills on time. I am uncomfortable paying slow. I will drive across town to pay back $20 I owe a buddy. My credit is impeccable. I always pay my debts.

My business downturn was challenging for me because the person I had always been needed to step aside and adjust my standards around paying bills.

Don't get me wrong; I did not stiff anyone. Still, I did need to have some uncomfortable conversations with my vendors and tell them I could not immediately pay them what I owed. It was terrible. They did not deserve it, and they had added tons of value to my company over the years.

Letting a vendor know you are struggling and making significant changes puts them on notice. It gives you a strong position to negotiate better terms. The reason is simple; if you go out of business, they are left holding the bag. It is in their best interest to help you through this downturn.

Your vendors will not want to help you if you come to them desperate or without a plan. You need to put a turnaround plan in place before you convey any bad news so you can explain your proposal with confidence.

Tell them things are bad, but that you have a turnaround plan that will put the company back on solid footing and allow you to continue doing business with them for many years. Tell them you need their help to achieve the turnaround. You do not need to go into any specifics on what your turnaround plan is, just explaining that you have one and they play an important role is enough.

Could you ask your landlord for a reduction in rent for six months? Could you ask for lower fees or get better payment terms from vendors? Can you reduce the hours you are paying to contractors or consultants? Could you give phantom equity instead of payment, or barter your products or services instead of paying cash? There are endless ways of getting help from the companies with whom you do business.

If you owe banks or other lending institutions, you may be able to reduce the amount that you owe, get a short payment deferral, or negotiate better payment terms. If you go out of business, the lender receives $0, so they may be willing to negotiate. Ask for their help. Until you ask, the answer will always be "no."

Cut Expenses in Phases

My suggestion in cutting expenses is to cut so deep that you will not have to come back later and cut more. Doing it once will give you extra cash runway to focus on building the company up, not the negative experience of cutting expenses over and over.

Despite my suggestions, however, you will most likely find yourself cutting expenses in phases. Here are some of the phases of cost-cutting I went through in my turnaround:

Phase 1–We are in trouble. We cut many expenses and felt there were only a few more that could still be cut and keep the company intact. We laid off about 20% of the employees, those who probably should have gone before the downturn.

Phase 2–Oh crap, it's worse than I thought. During this phase we cut even deeper on expenses, and this round hurt a lot more. We laid off even more employees, including managers and people that had been with us for five or more years.

Phase 3–This is really serious; we may not make it! Phase 3 was when we started to restructure the business model and removed some of our revenue channels that were not as profitable. We reduced the size of several departments within the company and got rid of some functions completely (the IT department was outsourced, for example). Phase 3 included a larger round of layoffs which was really tough.

Phase 4–When will this ride be over? In this phase, we had to go back to our yellow expenses and cut everything leftover. Even some significant green expenses were moved to red and cut, such as shutting down the office and finding outsourced fulfillment. We had to stop paying some of our bills (forced expense reduction). It was ugly.

Phase 5—I can see the light at the end of the tunnel. Finally, the forecast P&L looked stronger, and the monthly losses were trending down. There were no more cuts to be made, and we were down to just a handful of employees. We were super-efficient and only working on the most profitable activities. Profitability was within reach.

I hope you do not need to do four rounds of cost-cutting and that your turnaround is faster than mine.

Don't be surprised if you need to come back to your color-coded expense sheet and find a way to cut a little further.

You may be able to avoid some of this by making your cuts deeper the first time around. Cut fast and cut deep.

With each phase of cuts at Survival Frog, I honestly thought it was the last round of cuts and believed that it was not possible to cut any further. But as I discovered, there is always more to cut away.

Unless you can start increasing profitable revenue, you will have to reduce your expenses and labor costs to meet your new revenue level.

We tried our best to increase revenue, but it kept sliding lower and lower. So, we had to cut our expenses further and further.

Where does the expense cutting end? It ends when your revenue stabilizes, and you cut enough expenses to reach breakeven. If that revenue number keeps moving lower, then the cutting must continue.

Eventually, you may have a skeleton company where it is just you and a few employees. Although this may sound horrible to you, it may still produce enough money to live on, and you can start to rebuild over time.

I share the "phases" concept with you to encourage you to cut deep enough that you do not have to keep coming back to the cost-cutting measures. Realize that, no matter how deep you feel you reduce expenses, you may need to go back and cut more.

Chapter 21: Action Steps

- ➤ Create your color-coded spreadsheet, listing the reds you can cut first, the greens you can never cut, and rank the yellow "maybe" items in order of those most capable of cutting soon.
- ➤ How deep can you cut now? Go 20% more than that!

SECTION FOUR: CUTTING EXPENSES
AND FINDING EFFICIENCIES

CHAPTER 22
FINDING EFFICIENCIES
AND SIMPLIFYING

Simplify. ~Unknown

In a downturn, cutting expenses is not enough. You also need to find and implement new business efficiencies to streamline your operations.

It is likely you will be letting some employees go, and you cannot expect your remaining employees to double their working hours. You need to find efficiencies so you can get things done with fewer people.

With Survival Frog, we discovered and upgraded so many inefficiencies that you would not even recognize the new company's operations had you seen the previous version.

Almost everything changed, although some areas transformed more than others. The downturn and the sequential turnaround completely changed Survival Frog for the better. We now run on a fraction of employees as we had before, and the operation is smoother than ever.

The most significant changes for Survival Frog happened in three key areas of the company, the IT department, fulfillment, and the accounting department.

We found massive efficiencies in all these areas, which allowed us to get the job done with fewer people and lower expenses.

Your company may have different areas in need of improvement, but you can still learn from what I went through as encouragement for your turnaround.

IT Department

Our technology department (IT) was an area I knew little about before the downturn. I employed three people to run our IT projects and just assumed everything was running smoothly. However, during our turnaround, we discovered massive inefficiencies and wasted money.

Since Survival Frog was ten years old at the time, we had ten years of technology layers that we had to disassemble.

Each time a new IT manager was hired, they started their own projects and processes without cleaning up what the previous manager had done. This left a big mess that just kept accumulating over time.

We were paying for software that we had not ever used, and in some cases, did not even know what its function was. We found $2,000 worth of hosting servers running that did nothing.

What we found was downright embarrassing.

We had always had a big IT department and felt that the projects we were working on were essential. Only now can I see the waste we were putting up with and how all those critical projects simply were not that important to our survival.

Once we removed our complicated direct response revenue channel and decided to simplify our IT efforts, we were able to cut our bloated IT payroll of $25,000 per month to near $0. We had to give up most of our IT projects, but it forced us to simplify everything which helped us focus our efforts in other areas of the company. We eliminated the entire IT Department and paid an IT contractor a few hours per week to handle our technology needs.

I would have never thought I could revamp our IT department. It was a massive project, and I did not have a clue what I was doing. When I tell you there were tough days, that would be putting it mildly. Dealing with the security issues and disassembling the technology stack was so out of my comfort zone.

There were days of sheer terror and fear as we fired the IT manager and started peeling away the layers. When your back is against the wall and shutting down the business is the only other option, you make it work. You take it day by day and push through it.

Hindsight is 20/20, and I am confident you will eventually have some expenses that you will look back at and wonder why you ever felt they were important to keep.

Fulfillment Center

In Chapter 20, I shared with you how we outsourced warehousing and fulfillment operations to a third-party logistics company (3PL). It was a tough decision because we valued having the ability to fulfill our orders in-house.

After analyzing the costs associated with maintaining in-house fulfillment, we ultimately decided shutting it down was the right move to make. The savings were immense, and the disruption to our customers was minor.

Once our in-house fulfillment center and warehouse were gone, it was a no brainer to go virtual with the rest of the employees, allowing us to cut away even more overhead.

Accounting Department

I was never that comfortable with accounting or financial reports, but I was forced to dive into the financials when the business started to stumble. I had to learn what got us into trouble and find the way forward.

Accounting was yet another department that once I started pulling back the layers, I discovered it was sorely inefficient. Before the downturn, we had three full-time employees in accounting and were considering adding another.

I often did not get the monthly financial statements until 60+ days after the month-end. There were mistakes and inconsistencies everywhere. With my accounting department already struggling, the thought of firing everyone and starting over was scary.

Do not be surprised if your accounting department is in a similar situation. If you have been in business for more than five years and have not overhauled your accounting department recently, then you may have a large cost savings in this area.

Accounting technology has come a long way in a short time, and there are now ways to improve accuracy, find efficiencies, and lower your costs.

Not long ago, accountants in green visors poured over thick ledgers, manually adding columns of figures all day long.

Things have improved light-years since then, but Survival Frog's accounting department was still way too manual and slow.

I was able to cut our accounting department down from three employees to half an employee. No, I did not cut her in half. She spends the other half of her time in purchasing.

We accomplished this leap in efficiency by moving to an online accounting platform and using other applications for bill-pay, payroll, and timekeeping. We then used software connections to automate nearly all the accounting work.

The automation of our accounting department not only improved our bottom line, but I can see that bottom line faster! While it took 60 days or more to close our books before the automation, we can now get them done in under 15 days.

My reporting is better than ever now–I get weekly cashflow forecasts and do P&L forecasting right in our Operating Budget report.

In addition to cutting $15,000 in labor expense from the monthly budget, we now get our books faster and more accurately. I highly recommend you take a hard look at your accounting department and see where the waste is. It will pay off on your bottom line and speed up your turnaround.

If your accounting department has not undergone a major restructure in the last 5 years, then there is likely some major savings you can find in this area.

Reducing the size of the company

You probably realize that your business will need to look different to become ultra-efficient. In most cases, this means a smaller company, one that is "lean and mean."

That is not easy for an optimistic entrepreneur to do. After all, you want your turnaround to bring about a rebound in sales, so reducing the company's size is a hard pill to swallow.

Survival Frog became much more productive once we shrank in size. Take a look at Table 22-01 to see our labor efficiency ratio before and after the turnaround:

	Pre-Downturn	After Turnaround
Annual Revenue	$9,000,000	$3,000,000
Number of Employees	27	5
Labor Effeciency ($ per Employee)	$333,000	$600,000

Table 22-01

Our revenue dollar per employee almost doubled after the turnaround as we transformed the company to be ultra-efficient.

Making your company smaller forces you to find ways of being more efficient:

- Smaller office (or no office)

- fewer managers
- smaller staff
- fewer projects
- fewer (unprofitable) revenue channels
- fewer time-consuming data reports
- and more.

All these efficiencies add up to creating a lean and mean company that produces profits.

I suspect there is a smaller, more profitable company hiding inside the bloated big company you have become. If you strip away all the inefficiencies, all the expenses and, (gulp) the big staff, you will find the healthy and profitable company within.

Consider the idea of reducing the size of your company for the next 6 months. It could be the recipe for success in a downturn.

Your Role in Finding Efficiencies and Simplification

"Byron," you might be thinking, "How am I going to rebuild my IT department or an accounting department? I know nothing about that."

You are right. It is super intimidating. I get it because I am not an accounting person or an IT person. Yet, I was able to completely revamp those two departments.

The fact that I was not an expert in these areas worked in

my favor. I was not part of the accounting or IT department day-to-day operations, so I did not have any bad habits. I looked at the problems with a different set of eyes. I did not have any preconceived notions as to what was possible and what was not. I just knew we had to change.

Your job as the owner or CEO is to understand the most critical moving parts of any department. You do not need to know everything about an area of business, just the high-level moving parts.

I did not need to know everything about the IT department, I just had to know enough to be able to hire people that could help us rebuild. It was my role to not only find the efficiencies but to develop the master plan for each department's transformation.

A word of caution; relying on your current department manager to come up with the way forward can be challenging. Remember that this is the person that helped you get to the place you are now.

It is unlikely they can be the one to find a new way out.

There are too many previous decisions they will feel they must defend. Sometimes there is too much history to find your way forward. For this reason, you need to be the person who approves and pushes forward all major initiatives in your turnaround plan.

If you encounter resistance from your department managers, this could be a sign of trouble. The turnaround is hard enough as is, you do not want an old manager trying to pull you back into the old way of doing things.

We have talked a lot about cutting costs but cutting is not enough. Laying off employees is not enough. To survive a downturn and come out with a stronger company you also need to focus your efforts on becoming more efficient. This is the job for the owner or CEO of the business.

You need to get more done with fewer resources. This may include shrinking the company's size. The changes are painful to go through, but once you get to the other side you have a far better company. Take a deep breath and have faith that your turnaround plan will work. You've got this.

The Anticipation is So Much Worse Than the Action.

Nobody enjoys cutting expenses or simplifying a business. If you have made it through this section, I congratulate you.

As someone who has been through what you are going through, I can appreciate the fear and anxiety you will face before reducing expenses or staff. It can be terrifying.

As you work through your color-coded spreadsheet, you will speculate over what could go wrong and play out the worst-case scenarios repeatedly. In reality, the anticipation is the worst part.

The actual day you make those cuts is bad too, but somehow, it is not as bad as you thought it would be. In fact it feels a little better once you have pulled off the bandage.

After a few days you will feel good about it. You will start to look back and see all the worst-case scenarios that played out in your head were overblown and would never come to pass. The weight of huge monthly overhead costs has been lifted from your shoulders. You feel liberated.

Even when you lay off employees there is a period where your dominant thought is "why didn't I do that earlier?".

You have made progress and accomplished something significant. The forward momentum feels great and you have the energy to tackle the next hurdle.

The most considerable expense for most companies is labor. The fastest way to reduce your costs is to cut labor, which we have only touched on in this section.

The thought of laying off employees comes with a lot of emotions, baggage, and fear. In the next section, we will dissect this volatile topic so that you can approach it rationally and save your company without losing your sanity.

Chapter 22: Action Steps

➤ Are there any departments that you can restructure to run more efficiently or at a much lower cost? Even if the idea scares you, journal your thoughts on restructuring. You may not act on each idea, but the exercise will provide you with an outline of some significant changes if it comes to that.

SECTION FIVE
FINDING LABOR
EFFICIENCIES

Letting employees go is really, really hard–but you should be grateful that it's so hard. If it ever becomes easy, that is when you should be concerned. ~Byron

Letting employees go is one of the worst parts of any downturn. It causes sleepless nights, damages friendships, and dumps a mountain of guilt on any good leader's shoulders.

But here is the thing–be glad that it is such a horrible experience. Don't yearn for it to become easy one day.

Only a mean and heartless person would enjoy the process of letting employees go. Assuming you are someone who cares about your employees, this part of the journey will suck. This section of the book is here to make it suck less.

Finding labor efficiency is not just about firing people or reducing your labor expenses. Finding the perfect labor balance for your company almost always includes adding new team members and in Chapter 27 we discuss how best to add new rockstar employees to your team. Often removing an old manager and bringing in someone with a fresh perspective is the winning receipt for your turnaround.

Finding labor efficiency for your company will put you "in the zone." Your labor expenses will match your revenue and fixed cost structure to produce a highly profitable company. When you are in the labor efficiency zone you will also find your employees are the most resourceful and ultra-efficient with their time. It is the perfect balance of too much work, but all the important things are still getting done.

The most important thing to keep in mind while laying off employees during a downturn is that you are choosing the lesser of two evils. If you do not streamline your company and reduce staff during this rough patch, you may go out of business. If that happens, everyone loses their job, including you. By letting a few people go now, you can save the company and rebuild it.

In Chapter 19, we discussed how cutting expenses is the fastest way back to a profitable business. The $1:$1 ratio of cutting costs will impact the bottom line the most. Unlike additional revenue, for every dollar of labor expense you cut, $1 is directly added to your bottom line.

It is essential to remember the #1 goal during your turnaround, which is to **save the business**. While it is important to take care of your employees and try to provide financial security, it is not as crucial as the #1 goal. Do not lose sight of your most important job as the owner of your business. You must keep the business running, and this often requires some difficult decisions on your part.

To help you remember your #1 priority (to save your company), I've created the next page just for you.

The next time you are faced with an impossibly hard decision you can take a deep breath and refer to this page.

Next time you must fire a friend, make large cuts in the company or call a vendor to delay payment–you can look at this page.

This is a reminder that you must make difficult decisions and continue towards your #1 goal. Go ahead and rip the next page out and tape it to your wall.

SECTION FIVE: FINDING LABOR EFFICIENCIES

Your #1 Goal is…

To Stay in Business

CHAPTER 23
THE EMOTIONAL
ROLLERCOASTER

Sometimes being pushed to the wall gives you the momentum necessary to get over it! ~Peter de Jager

Before Survival Frog's downturn, we had 27 employees. When the turnaround was complete, there were only five people. It was brutal.

These were employees who had been with me for many years, some for over five years. I knew their families; I knew their kids' names and the sports they played. Letting people like that go is agonizing.

I had many sleepless nights and near panic attacks as I contemplated my next moves with employees. Without a doubt, I would say it was the hardest part of the Survival Frog turnaround.

Please understand that as you read this section, I may sound callous and removed of emotional sensitivity as I tell you to quickly lay off employees, but I completely understand the emotional roller coaster you are going through. I have been through it many times over.

Look upon my recommendations in this chapter the same way you would a friend giving you the raw advice you need to hear. I have no doubt you will layer in the humanity behind your difficult decisions. Since I do not know you personally (or your employees, or their children…) I am just going to tell it like it is.

Highs & Lows

A business owner preparing to lay off or fire staff will go through a roller coaster of emotions. It is something like being bipolar. There are ups and downs, highs and lows. Your thoughts will swing wildly from one direction to another.

One moment you know that letting an employee go is the best decision for them, the department, and the company. The next day, you swing the opposite way and second guess the decision. You create stories in your head predicting the demise of the company without the employee. Or your guilt spikes and, suddenly, the well-being (or lack thereof) of the employee is your main concern. The wild fluctuations in the stories you tell yourself are enough to make you crazy.

This rollercoaster of emotions is a normal part of the journey. Just knowing these emotional swings exist will help you work through them better.

The numbers do not lie and despite your vacillating thinking, you know the underlying objective must be to cut your labor expenses. Nevertheless, as lay off day draws closer, the more creative and demanding the stories you tell yourself become–pulling your heartstrings, keeping you up at night, and layering on the guilt.

The Stories You Will Tell Yourself

While the stories your mind whispers to you late at night may take many shapes, there are prevailing themes to the tales. Allow me to describe some of the most common assertions you will hear in your thoughts and provide some rational retorts.

I hope that reading about these "stories" will help you navigate past them. I do not expect you to dismiss the stories altogether, but at least you will recognize them faster and have additional ideas for dealing with them.

Story #1–I do not have time to cover the employee's work.

"Sure," you are probably saying, "I will save money, but that puts more work on my plate. I am already working 80 hours a week. The math does not work out. How can I cut staff if the work is going to land on me or on someone else who is equally maxed out?"

It can be hard to see now, but I assure you that you will find efficiencies and find a way to get their work done. At Survival Frog, I had employees spending 20 hours on something that, when I took it over, I was able to get the job down to five hours through finding efficiencies. Then I would delegate that five hours.

It is not that the employee was purposely inefficient, but as the owner, you know which parts of an employee's tasks are mission-critical, and which tasks can wait or be eliminated.

When things go back to normal, you can always add the responsibilities back in, but you are in crisis mode right now. Your goal is to make it through the downturn. You will find a way to cut those hours without piling another 40 hours onto your plate.

Remember that the *work always expands to fill the time given*. If you give it fewer hours, you will find there is less work. Have the faith that what must get done will still get done, and the efficiency you find will help your company in many ways.

Story #2–If I take over that work, I will be working "in the business" instead of "on the business."

It took me over five years to get out of the day to day at Survival Frog and work "on" growing my business. I vowed never to go back to performing the day-to-day work. However, I am grateful that I jumped back in and it was extremely healthy for my company.

If you are in a similar situation then it can be tough to start working "in" the business again. You are in crisis mode, however. You do what it takes to save the company, and that means you have to roll up your sleeves and work in the business for a few months. Think of this time as just taking one step back so you can move forward.

Working in the business during crisis mode has some benefits. It gives you a chance to re-organize your departments to be more efficient. Your employees, as good as they are, have probably not organized things well. You will often find that they have not put enough processes or training documents in place.

You can get in there as the owner and find many efficiencies. You may find a less expensive or even a free way to do something. You may find that a certain task is not needed anymore. It is rare for employees to detect the solutions that you, as the owner, can find.

You are viewing the job with a different perspective. That enables you to adapt the situation to be more efficient and effective. Once the downturn is over you can delegate that work and go back to working "on the business" once again.

Story #3—I do not know how to do the specific task.

This story takes on many forms:

"The employee knows so much. No one else knows how to do their work. It is not documented so it is all in their heads. Without them, we won't be able to operate the business smoothly."

Another common scenario:

"I used to know how to do the job, but the company has grown, and the position has changed. Now I don't even know what they do."

This objection is a big hurdle. Jumping back into the day-to-day operation after a significant passage of time is scary. The job's role has likely changed, and technology upgraded so much that you do not even know where to begin.

As the owner, you will find that you can learn how to run a department surprisingly fast. Google it, watch YouTube videos, and talk to friends who are experts in the field. Again, you do not have to know 100% of the function, but enough to create an efficient structure with the new labor restrictions.

You may not know how to do their job now, but you will very quickly figure it out. Once you do, you will discover there were so many areas of improvement that the previous employee simply overlooked.

Story #4—The employee has critical relationships with our top clients who will leave if I fire the employee. Worse, the employee may steal our customers away.

This story can be terrifying and may also contain some truth, so tread lightly. I have seen several friends go through this situation with their B2B clients, but I have found that it always seems much worse than what it turns out to be.

As the owner, you should stay in contact (at least quarterly) with your top clients. If you have not done this in the past, that is okay, but start now. Your personal relationship with the client can save the situation when you need to let a key employee go.

Having strong employment agreements that address the issue of ex-employees poaching your top customers will help reduce the risk in this area. You do not have employment agreements? Here is your wake-up call to get them in place with all your key employees.

Regardless of whether you have employment agreements in place or have personal relationships with your top clients, your business should never be held hostage by one employee. It is time to take back control. Even if you lose a customer's business, it is entirely possible that the net savings from letting the employee go still puts you ahead of the game.

Story #5—My employee will not land on their feet; this layoff will devastate them.

This story can quickly spin out of control as your mind plays out all possible doomsday scenarios. Nevertheless, the reality I have seen over and over is that past employees always find their way.

Your responsibility is to save the company; their responsibility is to provide for their family. Let that separation play out and allow them to figure out their own life challenges.

In most cases, I have seen employees go on to do bigger and better things. Many go on to find higher paying jobs or move on to start their own business. Have faith that they will find their way. They always do.

Story #6—The rest of my team will see this and start looking for new jobs, so this will hurt employee morale.

Depending on who from your team is let go, you may or may not see an initial hit on your company's morale. However, my experience is that, like many of the stories we tell ourselves, this will not be as big of an issue as you imagine it will be.

If played right, I found that layoffs can create a positive effect on company spirit. I had many concerns over employee morale, so I was proactive and had companywide meetings immediately after a layoff, whether it was one employee or a large group.

In most cases, I discovered that the rest of the team rallied behind the decisions and saw the situation as an opportunity to fix the company and improve their standing within the company.

For some employees that I let go, the feedback was very positive, as in: "that should have happened a long time ago."

Story #7–They may go rogue and try to sabotage the company.

The thought of an ex-employee going on a rampage to undermine your company is terrifying. Let me ask you this: if you have someone that would make an effort to hurt you and the company after losing their job, why would you want them working for your company? My recommendation is to get them out the door as soon as possible.

A slight variation on this story is when an ex-employee starts up a competing business, and you fear what that will do to your company. Even if you have an agreement with the employee that specifically prohibits them from competing with your company, in all honesty, those non-compete agreements are difficult to enforce. All you can really do is go on with your business and do a better job running it than they will theirs.

Story #8–I cut their department or project, but I can keep them busy somewhere else.

This noble thought is common but dangerous to your turnaround efforts. If, to ensure your business's health, you are simplifying your business by eliminating company functions, you need to finish the job and cut all the labor expense related to the restructuring.

It is always possible to find extra work for someone to do within your company. However, I caution you to not fall into that trap.

To realize the full impact of restructuring a department, you need to cut deep. Do not fall into the trap of "finding extra work" for someone that needs to go. Cut the expense and let them go.

The stories and mind tricks I have shared in this section are rarely as our minds suggest they will be. I could give you 100 rational responses to any story your head throws at you. Unfortunately, we are not dealing with reason here.

The stories you invent in the middle of the night are mind games, plain and simple. Your subconscious mind is trying to protect you from the pain it anticipates on that terrible day you cut the employees loose.

The stories will barge into your head when you are most vulnerable and try to persuade you away from doing what is best for your company. Just recognize those mind games when they come crashing in, and even if the stories have a grain of truth to them, do not let that alter your plans to lower labor expenses.

The Roller-Coaster Ride Continues

When you get past all the self-doubt and mind-stories, it is finally time to pull the trigger and let the employee(s) go. Even then, the rollercoaster ride continues.

By far, the worst part of the layoff process is leading up to the day you implement the layoffs. The actual day you let the employee go is bad, but as time progresses, it gets significantly better.

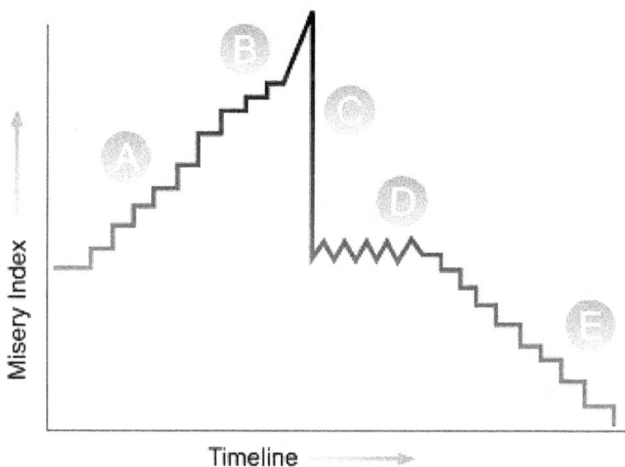

This graph demonstrates the emotional rollercoaster you will probably experience.

A–The lead up to the day you implement the layoffs is full of mini-ups and downs, self-doubt, and stories playing continually in your mind. It gets progressively worse as you make the final decisions and the actual day approaches.

B–There is high anxiety on the day before and the day of the layoffs.

C–The next day, it is as though a heavy load has been lifted off your shoulders. The rollercoaster ride is not over, and you feel awful about what has transpired, but you have gotten through the worse of it.

D–This is when you figure out how to get the job done without the person working in your company, and you begin experiencing the inevitable pains of getting more done with fewer people.

E–Once the duties have been re-assigned and you have found significant efficiencies in the tasks; it gets much more comfortable. You may even start finding skeletons in the closet and learn that the laid-off employees were not doing that great a job after all. That helps justify your decision, and you feel even better about your choice.

I understand that your mind is playing tricks on you and making you believe that you cannot possibly let your staff go. However, I promise you that once you rip off the bandage and figure out how to run the company without the extra employees, it goes much smoother than you ever anticipated.

Chapter 23: Action Steps

➤ Have you felt the swing in thoughts regarding letting employees go? What "stories" are you telling yourself? True or false, write those notes in your turnaround journal.

CHAPTER 24
PREPARING FOR LAYOFFS

Dealing with employee issues can be difficult, but not dealing with them can be worse. ~Paul Foster

No Surprises

I have made many mistakes firing or laying off employees over the years. Probably the biggest mistake I ever made, and the one I vowed never to repeat, is when I did not make it evident to the employee beforehand what was coming.

If you have an employee that you need to fire for poor job performance, there should be negative performance reviews and official "corrective action" write-ups. They need to know what is coming. If an employee is genuinely surprised at being fired, you must have missed some critical steps along the way.

In the area of layoffs, there are several warning shots you can fire before the dreaded day. At Survival Frog, I made it extremely clear to the staff that the company was struggling.

We had company-wide meetings where I explained that we were losing money and that significant changes were coming. I would focus these "big changes" around all the expenses we were cutting, such as software, canceling employee retreats, or expensive holiday dinners. Some of the cut expenses were small, like no more snacks in the breakroom, but it sent a big message.

Nevertheless, I recommend you never openly state that layoffs are coming. That would be too much. By showing all the other areas where you are restricting spending, employees can read between the lines and see that labor expenses could be next.

If you have been transparent with the company's financial situation and announced various expense reduction measures along the way, your employees should not be greatly surprised to see layoffs.

The employees are probably more prepared for the inevitable than you anticipate. Unless they have been working under a rock, they have been sensing uncertainty as well. Divulging the truth will bring relief and the chance to start making other plans.

For this reason, it is critical that you communicate to your top performers, the ones you are most likely to keep after layoffs, that your plans are to keep them with the company. They will need assurance from you.

The Math Behind Layoffs

Any time you need to let an employee go from your company, you experience a tidal wave of emotions. Now is when the logic and math behind your decisions can help you. I am not suggesting you strive to be heartless and focus only on the numbers but do let logical business decisions help lead you to the right verdict.

Let's dive into a few ways to use logical decisions to justify layoffs.

Reduction by restructuring

Throughout this book, we have stressed the benefits of restructuring your company. That includes potentially cutting revenue channels or even entire departments if that is what is required to reach optimization.

At Survival Frog, we had to restructure several departments, and in doing so we were able to reduce labor costs significantly. That is an example of a reduction by restructuring.

It is not only expenses and labor costs you need to reduce; there are also projects that will need to be eliminated. Be sure to look at projects that are not currently producing profit. During your turnaround it is critical to eliminate the labor associated with non-performing or under-performing projects.

Reduction by poor performance

I have discovered that my highest-performing employees are often two or three times more productive than the worst-performing employees. That is 200-300% more work done every day by the superstars than by those that are not performing up to standards.

Not all employees can perform at superstar levels, but make sure the employees you keep around are not dragging down your efficiency. By letting go of employees who do not perform well, you reduce your labor costs and create a culture of excellence and high efficiency.

You may not realize how efficient or inefficient an employee is until you put someone new into their position who gets significantly more work done in less time. Short of that measurement, however, I have found that the best indicator of inefficient or slow employees is to look for the turmoil and mistakes.

Where you see smoke, there is usually fire. Where you discover employees making mistakes, causing drama, or creating other problems, you will most likely find the opportunity for significant efficiency.

During a downturn, you may need to let go some of your best employees due to budget constraints, so letting go of an employee not living up to your company's standards is a no brainer. Cutaway the shoddy performers first. This will have a surprisingly positive effect on your company's morale.

Create a list of all employees that you know are not the best fit for the company, the culture, or their position. Be very honest with yourself and ask yourself if you would hire them again. Acknowledge that, even if you were not in a downturn, they probably should be let go regardless. Then let them go.

Reduction by budget constraints

A friend recently asked me, "How do I know when to stop laying off employees?"

For most small businesses, the answer is simple: When you stop losing money.

After you complete layoffs based on performance and restructuring, you may think (hope) you are done. However, if your forecasted P&L's still do not show a profit after those initial cuts, you may need to reduce your labor expenses even further.

There is a concept in accounting called "cost creep," where a company's costs and expenses creep up over time. The same concept of cost creep may, in fact, be even more common in the labor expense category. "Labor creep" happens when you hire new people to solve problems, instead of dealing with the core problems.

Over time your team becomes less efficient. It can take a significant downturn to see how far labor creep has slithered through your company. Budget constraints will force your hand to, once again, become an efficient operation.

Forecast new labor expenses

Once you have determined that reducing labor cost must be part of your turnaround plan, it is now time to dive into the numbers to see how far you need to cut.

Your P&L will show you the way. The art of forecasting your P&L is where the turnaround takes place. Your next exercise is to calculate how much you must reduce your labor expenses under various scenarios based on different revenue levels, margins, and expense reductions.

At the point where all these fluctuating numbers show a profit (or at least breakeven), you will find the required level of labor cuts.

When analyzing your labor costs be sure you are doing the math correctly. Each person on your team costs more than just their salary or hourly rate. They might earn paid time off (PTO), bonus pay, and health insurance as well. Then add taxes you pay on their behalf, 401K contributions, or other HR-related costs. The employee probably requires computers, equipment, software licenses, and other work-related tools. An employee who makes $20 per hour might save you $25 or more per hour if you let them go.

Labor efficiency ratio

Another useful tool to analyze your labor costs and to find optimum employee levels is the Labor Efficiency Ratio.

The best accounting book I have found for non-accountants is *Simple Numbers* by Greg Crabtree. Crabtree makes the complicated topic of running a business using financial metrics and makes it easy for entrepreneurs to understand. In his book, Crabtree explains the concept of labor productivity, salary caps, and the labor efficiency ratio.

The idea behind **Labor Efficiency Ratio (LER)** is simple; your total labor costs should not exceed a predetermined ratio of your gross revenue. Look at the example on Table 24-01 below.

Gross Revenue	$500,000	
COGS	-$200,000	40%
Non-Labor Expenses	-$100,000	20%
Labor Expenses	-$150,000	30% (LER)
Net Profit	**$50,000**	**10%**

Table 24-01

Assuming COGS is optimized and your non-labor expenses are low and efficient, you can expect that if your LER is 30% or lower, you will have 10% profitability.

If your LER goes above 30%, then your company will realize less profit. If you can drive the LER down to 25%, your profitability will be higher.

LER is most powerful once you determine the range it should stay within. Every business is different, and it may take some time for you to determine what your perfect LER range is.

If your LER range is between 25% and 30%, then you will have upper and lower limits where decisions should be made. As you move in on the 25% ratio, you will see more profits come into the company. When you dip below that 25% LER ratio, this can be your indicator to hire more people or expand an area of your company.

When you approach the 30% LER ratio this is an alarm bell that your labor costs are too high for your current revenue levels. This is when you need to consider reducing your employee count. An example is on Table 24-02 on page 243.

Before I started using the LER concept at Survival Frog, we would hire new employees anytime we had "too much work" and not enough people. Makes sense, right? No!

Once Survival Frog started monitoring the LER and using a range to determine when to hire or fire, we stopped hiring new people on a whim. That forced us to find new efficiencies and hire only when the LER was below the predetermined percentage.

	It's Time To Hire		It's Time To Fire	
Gross Revenue	$500,000		$500,000	
COGS	-$200,000	40%	-$200,000	40%
Labor Expenses	-$110,000	22% (LER)	-$165,000	33% (LER)
Non-Labor Expenses	-$100,000	20%	-$100,000	20%
Net Profit	$90,000	18%	$35,000	7%

Table 24-02

There are different variations of LER that you can use. You can use labor as a percentage of net profit instead of gross revenue. Or you could monitor the profit in dollars per full-time employee. Alternatively, you can simply assert that the company will only hire once it has reached a certain pre-determined net profit percentage.

Whatever variation of the LER you choose to track and monitor your labor costs, the concept is the same: looking at a ratio range, and only hiring or firing when you fall outside your prearranged "healthy" range.

The LER helps you take the emotions out of your labor decisions and use hard data to support your determination. That will ultimately help you to run a more efficient company.

Let the numbers help you through tough decisions. Set ratios and acceptable ranges for hiring or firing employees and stick to them. Following that practice allows you to create a highly profitable company that can survive any future market downturn.

Organization Chart

One last strategy for reducing the emotional rollercoaster in laying off employees is to create an organizational chart. You may already have one, but in all likelihood, it is nothing like the kind I will suggest in this section.

I have found the best "org charts" are handwritten, so start with that. When you have something finalized you can add it to a mind mapping software, so you have pretty circles and arrows.

Here is your step-by-step outline for creating your new organizational chart:

Step 1–Forget every organizational structure you have done in the past. Your goal is to redesign your company. Start by putting your name as the owner or CEO at the top of the chart. Then diagram your largest departments that report directly to you.

Step 2–Determine how many full-time employees (FTE) you can afford, using your forecasted P&L figures or LER percentages. That is the maximum number of FTE you can have in your organizational chart.

Step 3–Decide where to add the FTE on your chart. Do not, (and I repeat), do not put anyone's names on the organizational chart. Just map out where the FTE should go. Be careful with your allotted FTE, and do not allocate more than you can afford. If one department historically had three FTE, and you do not have enough FTEs available, find a way to get the job done with only one or two.

Here is an example of an organization chart for a company that can only afford seven FTE:

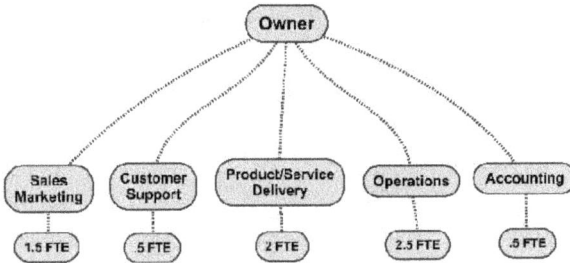

Covering Critical Tasks

Before letting an employee go you need to understand the tasks they are currently responsible for and which will need to be covered after they are gone. Making a list of all the duties, projects, and responsibilities that they have will help you see the big picture.

I cannot stress enough that after the list of responsibilities is complete, you should not feel that you must complete all the tasks moving forward. You will have "forced efficiency" once the employee has left the company. Only the most critical tasks need to be done.

You will find tasks or projects on your list that you decide can be placed on hold or disregarded entirely. For those must-do jobs, you now have the chance to find ways to create massive efficiencies related to the task.

Once you have a list of all activities the employee was working on, ask the question: "what can we stop doing moving forward?"

Simplify the position and only work on the tasks that are most critical. Where possible, place several of the tasks on hold for the next six months while you complete the turnaround, and then reassess their necessity.

Legal Considerations

Although most companies in the United States can hire and fire people at will, there are specific state laws that you will need to follow. This book cannot cover all the legal details you will need to know before effecting a layoff or firing someone.

Talk with an attorney and assess your risks before you let an employee go from your company. Have solid employment agreements and separation agreements. Know the laws regarding unemployment, health insurance, discrimination laws, and any other state or industry specifics that could get your company into trouble.

A friend of mine gave me some great advice many years ago relating to legal issues. For any issue that could present a legal risk, always "write it for the judge." This means all your communications should be written as if a judge will eventually be reading it in deciding the fate of your legal issues.

If anything happens with an employee that you could reasonably believe might end up in court someday, document the event as if a judge will review it at some point. That includes all emails, contracts, conversations, and more. Write it for the judge, and you will never have regrets down the road.

Documentation

Even when laying off employees for financial reasons, I suggest you keep separate documentation of any prior performance issues you had with an employee. If you lay off five employees and retain ten in the company, it is a good practice to have documented reasons why you chose those five employees to lay off.

Many times, if I want to document something officially, I simply send an email to another manager in the company, explaining the situation at hand. The email has a date and time stamp and can be referenced later if required.

Severance and separation agreements

Obtaining a Separation Agreement from an employee leaving the company is an effective way to reduce the risk of repercussions coming back at you in the future. It documents that the employee did not feel discriminated against or know of any inequity or wrongdoing on the part of the company when they signed the agreement.

While a separation agreement is not guaranteed to keep you out of hot water, it goes a long way.

A separation agreement can also include a list of equipment or documentation to be returned to the company, non-compete clauses, and even non-disclosure and non-disparagement language.

So why would an employee sign away most of their rights? Cash, in the form of severance pay.

A vital component of the separation agreement is an arrangement to provide severance pay to the departing employee. Check state and local laws for any requirements surrounding severance pay, as there may be a waiting period after the employee signs the agreement before the severance should be paid.

Paying out severance is a tool to soften the financial blow to the employees you are laying off. Although it is not legally required (unless built into a formal policy), it is a nice gesture for the employees that have been with you for a while.

I provided severance pay to most of the employees I let go during our downturn. The amount was not as much as it would have been if the company had been profitable, but I usually managed to give a couple weeks of severance. The longer the employee had been with the company, the more considerable the severance amount was.

The severance payment also helped to mitigate any employee retaliation that may have come our way. They signed the separation agreement, returned their equipment in good condition, and we parted on good terms.

Unemployment Insurance and COBRA

Typically, in a layoff situation, unemployment compensation is the employee's right. Even if you are firing the employee for cause or they offer to resign, there are ways of structuring their departure so they can still get help from unemployment benefits.

If you are forced to let several employees go from your company, you may see your unemployment insurance increase over the next year. However, this is typically a small cost, and it provides a tremendous service to your employees that leave the company.

If you offer health insurance, you will need to provide payment logistics for COBRA insurance. The employee pays for COBRA insurance, but in some states, the company is responsible for the premium payments and must arrange for reimbursement from the ex-employee.

Witnesses

In subsequent sections, I will describe best practices for handling a layoff, but now I want to stress the importance of having another person witness the meeting where you let the employee go.

Your witness need not say a word as you break the bad news to the employee you are letting go. The role of the witness is to be a fly on the wall. Ask them for 15 minutes of their time and let them know they should not say anything. If the employee questions the witness, they should look to you to respond. Their role is merely to listen as a third-party observer.

It is not important who this person is, but that you have someone else in the room. After you have dismissed the employee and they have left the building, you should write the witness a short email outlining what transpired in the meeting. If the ex-employee behaved negatively during the meeting, request that the witness reply to your email with their impression of what transpired to document the encounter.

Departure List

Developing an off-boarding checklist will help smooth the departure of staff for both the employee and the company. Whenever you encounter an issue with a layoff or recognize something you should do differently next time, update the checklist accordingly.

The off-boarding checklist should include confirming the return of the employee's computer and other equipment and obtaining customer or vendor contact lists.

Ensure that you get the employee's new email address, phone number, and mailing address since you may need to contact them in the future.

Be sure to change all passwords and lock the departing employee out of the company software and technology infrastructure. Forward their company email address to their manager or yourself to handle any lingering business. Have the employee return the office key and change all security codes they may have used while employed with the company.

If there is an important project or help you need from them over the next few weeks, you may consider a contractual arrangement where you pay them an hourly rate for the work they perform.

While it is common for employees to give the company two weeks' notice when resigning, I have found it is almost impossible to get a laid-off employee to stay around the office for the next two weeks. They usually just want to cut bait and get out of there.

However, depending on the unique situation, you may want to offer to pay them an hourly rate to help with the transition, which could provide a little extra cash to them as they search for a new job.

Most states require a company to pay the employee promptly for their time worked, which may include unused PTO (paid time off). You can have a check waiting for them when you let them go. I usually mail it to the employee within a day, and include the entire last day of pay, even if I let them go in the morning.

The Third Time Is a Charm

The best advice I can give you regarding layoffs is to cut so deep you only need to do it once. However, you may need to come back to this task a few times.

One evening I was meeting with a business friend who asked me how my turnaround was going. I explained how we had just finished a second round of layoffs. I had to let ten people go and I was still shaken up by the day.

He paused, knowing I would not want to hear what he had to say next. "I don't know why it is," he said, "but the waves of layoffs always seem to come in threes."

He said it was a definite pattern amongst his clients, and he cautioned me that the third round would hurt most of all.

He was right.

The first round of letting employees go is often just clearing out people that should have been let go anyway. The downturn simply hastens the inevitable. The whole company breathes a sigh of relief when they no longer have to work with a square peg in a round hole.

Round two of the employee cuts takes place when the first attempt did not bring the P&L into profit territory as you had hoped. You must reduce your expenses further and labor is one of the biggest costs you have control over. This round is always much more painful, so be ready. You may need to sacrifice some of your managers, or a few up and coming employees. It will rock the boat, and it is going to hurt. This round may even leave "holes" in your company's workflow, and you will be forced to find new efficiencies to get the work done.

The third round is excruciating. You are letting some of your key players go and you may only be left with a skeleton staff. The third round is a drastic cut and will change the structure of your company, but the hope is that you can start rebuilding from there.

My friend correctly predicted my situation and I found myself doing a third and final layoff just a few months after our conversation. The three rounds of employee cuts are a common occurrence in a turnaround. It would make more sense to go through the pain of just one large layoff, but in reality, you may find yourself revisiting this task a third time.

Chapter 24: Action Steps

- ➤ What is the math telling you concerning your labor costs? Where do you feel you LER range should be?
- ➤ List all your employees and categorize them into three groups: (1) should be let go first, (2) harder to let go, and (3) the last few people you must keep.
- ➤ Forecast P&L statements with varying levels of labor reduction to see how deep you should cut.
- ➤ Create your "departure" list to avoid missing any crucial steps when laying off or firing employees.

CHAPTER 25
STEP BY STEP ON HOW
TO LET EMPLOYEES GO

The future starts today, not tomorrow. ~Pope John Paul II

Prepare Emotionally

Recall my advice at the beginning of this section. This experience is supposed to suck. And if it is not an awful experience for you, then you have other issues (such as being a real SOB).

During Survival Frog's downturn, I went through three painful rounds of layoffs, and each time was horrible.

There were other individuals I had to let go along the way, but there were three distinctive layoff days where I had to let a large chunk of our employees go.

I do not consider myself good at firing people, and it is not a skill I ever want to master. Honestly, my goal was to just get through the day without putting the company in legal jeopardy.

Your employee will need space and empathy, so prepare yourself to be patient and add grace to the conversation. Expect that the employee could respond differently than what you anticipate. It is an alarming and confusing time for them, and you will likely see a side of the person that you have never seen before.

Brace yourself to stay steady and mature, and not let your emotions take over. Remember that you are choosing the lesser of two evils by streamlining staff rather than slowly going out of business. It is your responsibility to let them go so that the company can move forward and, hopefully, employ others in the future.

I have read studies that report that terminated employees are usually more upset with *how* they were let go, than with the actual act of being let go. So be compassionate and mature about the situation and give them space to react.

Logistics

Before starting the departure meeting, you need to handle a few logistics. The standard recommendation is to let employees go on a Friday afternoon. I never really followed that principle and did it on the day that made the most sense for the company.

My main concern was to have as many remaining staff members still in the office so I could have a quick meeting explaining what just took place. That usually meant not waiting until the end of the day when some employees may have already left.

Schedule the layoff conversation in a private setting where the employee will have easy and fast access to leave if they decide to make a quick getaway.

Have tissues on the table nearby in case emotions run high.

Have your separation agreement printed and ready to give to the employee. My recommendation is not to accept a signed agreement until they have had time to review it later in private. They are too emotional and agitated during the meeting to grasp details and think clearly.

I have personally never had any security issues when letting someone go. Still, it is worth mentioning that if you have concerns over anyone's safety, you should take measures to ensure you protect everyone.

Arrange for your witness, as mentioned in Chapter 24, to be in the meeting room before the employee arrives, so there is no awkward wait time. Call the person you are letting go into the office or go to their desk and ask them to join you.

The Conversation

If you were expecting a long script to memorize, that is just not the case. Your goal is to cover the necessities and nothing more. Keeping this meeting short is your primary goal (and will help keep your sanity).

The entire meeting should not last more than five or ten minutes. In most cases, the employee wants to get out of that room just as desperately as you.

When doing group layoffs, I find it is best to do one-on-one meetings with each person.

Here is what I typically say:

Please come in, have a seat. I have asked (witness) to join us for this meeting.

It has been a tough decision, but we are letting you go effective today. As you know, the company has been struggling, forcing us to let you go. I am sorry things could not work out. (That is it, say nothing more here.)

We are planning on paying out severance to you in the amount of $____. This agreement spells everything out. I do not want you to sign it now but instead take it home to review. If everything looks good, then get it back to me, and we will pay out the severance after a ____day waiting period.

For the hours of work that we owe you, you will get a check tomorrow (or give them a check now). *We are paying you out for a full day of work today, but you can leave now.*

I'm sorry things didn't work out.

Then wait for their reaction. Ninety percent of the time I find that employees simply say they understand and you part ways. On occasion there are tears, and even more rare are upset emotions and anger. It is important that you do not over complicate this process and that you keep things short and to the point.

I have had my share of emotional situations when letting both men and women go. Allow them space to react but do not fan the flame with nervous talk.

Silence is okay; do not feel as if you need to keep a conversation going. Simply empathize with them and give them room to digest the situation.

Do Not Defend the Decision

Some of the most uncomfortable situations I have had to work through is when the employee tries to talk you out of the decision or asks for further reasoning why you are letting them go.

That is a trap; do not go down that path. Under no circumstances should you justify your decision, and in no way should you refer to their work performance.

Even if I am firing someone for poor performance, I will say: "I'm sorry, but it's just not working out, we're letting you go, effective today." That's it, nothing more.

Defending your reason for letting an employee go just leads to quibbling over details and rumors. It never goes well and does not lead anywhere good. Just explain "the decision has already been made, and we are letting you go, effective today. The decision is final."

If you feel so motivated to give them constructive feedback on their work performance, you can do that in a few weeks over coffee or a phone call. Today, your only task is to inform them of the decision.

You will never win a debate during an exit meeting, and it will drag the discussion on for entirely too long. Keep it short.

"The decision has already been made, and we're letting you go, effective today. The decision is final."

Hand them the prepared separation agreement and ask them to review it later. You must make it clear that nothing they say will change the situation.

Next Steps

You did it. It may not have been perfect, and it may have been tough, but you made it through the layoff. You are not entirely done, however. Now you need to communicate what just happened with the remaining team members and set the stage for the next step of your turnaround.

At this point in the day, you probably just want to run out of the office and head home (or to the bar). Or at least lock the door and not come out to see anyone else for a while.

Hiding in your office will only start the rumor mill going as the remaining employees invent stories far worse than reality.

As soon as the laid-off employees leave the building, announce a short team meeting with the remaining staff. The meeting should start immediately after the layoff, do not schedule it for later in the day.

It is your opportunity to control the narrative and to re-establish the company's turnaround plan. Remind the team that although this decision was tough, it is setting the company up for success.

At Survival Frog, the post-layoff staff meetings rallied the troops and left the remaining team members feeling like the chosen ones; entrusted with our company's survival.

A word of warning, however. The post-layoff staff meeting is not the time to share any negative feedback about the laid-off employee's performance, even if it was a factor in letting them go.

It is much more beneficial to frame it as the employee's choice or a mutual decision to part ways, if possible. Even if it was a disciplinary action, I always gave the departing employee the benefit of the doubt by keeping my communication positive.

Sympathize with the remaining employees, since many were friends with those that were laid off. Refocus on the turnaround plan and talk about the way forward.

This meeting is also the time you can discuss who is taking over responsibilities that the laid-off employees once held.

Although you will come to this meeting with a plan of action already, it is a good idea to get feedback from the team about which projects will be sidelined or paused, which actions will still need to be completed moving forward, and who is best to perform them?

Avoiding or delaying the post-layoff meeting with the rest of the team is dangerous. It is imperative that you make an appearance, give the bad news yourself, and then share your optimism for the turnaround plan and the way forward.

Chapter 25: Action Steps

> It's better to be prepared, so come up with a plan of action days or weeks before the big day. Review this chapter to make sure you are ready.

CHAPTER 26
OTHER WAYS OF CUTTING
LABOR EXPENSES

Those who attend to small expenses are always rich.
~ John Adams

Although employees make up most of your labor costs, this is not the only place to look. Here are a few other areas where you can find improved labor efficiency and cut additional expenses.

Contractors

Contract labor may be an area to focus on before you start any employee layoffs. Examine the contractors and consultants you use to determine if you can eliminate or minimize their tasks and trim those expenses.

Agency Relationships

Like contract labor, you can reduce or eliminate the agencies your company uses. In some cases, marketing agencies may be willing to reduce their fee structure or agree to a three or six-month pause while you regroup.

Compensation Changes

Depending on your type of company, there may be some opportunity to change how your employees are compensated. You could potentially ask your sales or marketing staff to take lower hourly or salary amounts in exchange for higher commission levels. That change could shift the motivation and place more emphasis on profitable revenue results.

Another potential idea is to reduce the entire staff's salary by 10 or 20% over the next few months. Before going down this path, be sure to forecast the financial impact it will have and make sure it is worth the disruption it may cause to your team.

Chapter 26: Action Steps

➢ Where else can you cut on labor costs, such as contractors, consultants, or agencies?

➢ Are there changes to employee compensation that could help temporarily reduce costs?

SECTION FIVE: FINDING LABOR EFFICIENCIES

CHAPTER 27
HOW TO HIRE GREAT PEOPLE

I hire people brighter than me and then I get out of their way. ~Lee Iacocca

You may wonder why I included the topic of hiring in this section about laying off your employees, but it is critically important for two reasons:

First, once your turnaround takes hold and you see your profits increase, you will need to add new team members to fill the gaps created during the previous downturn.

Secondly, and potentially even more critically, you may need to let go of some people and immediately hire replacements.

That may sound strange. Why would you let an employee go if you are just going to hire another person to their job? But this point is essential, so stick with me.

Fresh Eyes

I found when I was restructuring the departments at Survival Frog, I had to remove the old managers and get a set of "fresh eyes" on the problem before we could truly see progress.

It is difficult (almost impossible) for a manager who has been running an inefficient department for a few years to turn things around.

You may believe that the current manager can make changes to the department, but do not be fooled into believing that he or she now "gets it" and won't hang on to old beliefs.

If an employee has been with the company for a while, it is challenging for them to completely rip off the bandage and make massive changes all at once.

There is just too much history which causes hesitations in killing old projects and an unwillingness to restructure the company. There is a strong desire to justify their previous decisions and the work they have been focused on over the last few years.

A new manager does not have that baggage. They can see a situation for what it is and disband the old, inefficient ways of doing things.

I realize this is hard to hear, but to create a big turnaround, you will need a big change. Often the old guard is not able to create the change that is necessary.

You want someone to come in and not be tempted to resist change. You need someone with a different set of beliefs and experiences relating to a particular challenge.

The Survival Frog accounting department is a great example. It was so antiquated and inefficient; it should have been easy to find efficiencies. Instead we struggled to even identify the inefficiencies and thought what we were doing was the way it should be done.

We had to abolish the existing accounting department altogether and bring in fresh eyes to rebuild and find significant efficiencies.

Our accounting department has now been streamlined and automated to the point where what once took three full-time employees, we now get done with half an employee.

You need to add a few new members to your management team to stir the pot and create big change. You need to create a turnaround team.

A turnaround team moves quickly and does not get hung up on limited thinking. They certainly do not hold on to old projects they are emotionally tied to or feel they must justify. Your turnaround team should thrive from big changes. They need to rally behind the turnaround—for the sake of survival. Your management team must be more focused on action and the way forward—not what is behind them.

Another benefit in upgrading your team is it may even save you money. If you have a manager that has been with your company for several years, you most likely gave annual raises and may now be paying them at the top of the pay scale.

You may find that you can pay a new, hungry, and eager employee significantly less.

Envision lowering your labor cost while increasing the quality of your team. That would be quite a gain. The cost savings is welcome, but the real benefit is the fresh eyes and the efficiencies you will find.

It is tough to consider letting someone familiar go only to hire someone new, but the strategy is worth looking at seriously.

Upgrade Your Team

Of course, labor efficiency begins at the top, and one of your most critical jobs going forward will be to hire only the best employees.

There is one word to keep in mind when hiring people during or after a turnaround: Upgrade.

Once you have accomplished the incredible task of finding your labor efficiencies, you never again want to settle for less. You have seen what it takes to let go of C and B players, so now it is time to learn how to hire A-level players.

One of the best resources I have found for hiring rockstar employees comes from the book: *WHO*, by Geoff Smart and Randy Street. In this easy-to-read book, Smart and Street give a repeatable system for interviewing job candidates. By using highly effective interview questions and following the same format with each person, you can easily compare each candidate and see where the best culture and skill set matches are.

Using the approach outlined in the *WHO* book, we drastically upgraded Survival Frog's team. Everyone who works for us now is an incredible culture fit and has a strong work ethic.

Chapter 27: Action Steps

➢ Do you have any key employees that may be struggling to let go of pre-existing notions or are hung up on egos associated with past decisions?

➢ Get the *WHO* book by Geoff Smart and create a reliable hiring method, so you have confidence in finding top talent for your company.

SECTION FIVE: FINDING LABOR EFFICIENCIES

CHAPTER 28
COMMUNICATING THE
TURNAROUND
WITH YOUR TEAM

The single biggest problem in communication is the illusion that it has taken place. ~George Bernard Shaw

If you do not communicate with your team, your employees will come up with their own stories. The rumor mill will churn at full speed. The stories they come up with are almost always worse than reality. Control the narrative by giving regular updates to the entire team.

It is smart to determine how you will frame the turnaround to your staff ahead of time. Perhaps using words like "pivoting" or an "improvement plan" is a more encouraging and viable way of getting through the changes ahead.

You can put a positive spin on things by explaining the company is reducing its product or service offerings to give more attention to your best customers and top selling products. Even shutting down the office can be explained as the best way to streamline your efficiencies and provide employees with a better quality of life.

Different people in your company will no doubt be privy to varying levels of information. Your management team will need to be closer to the fire and help you solve critical issues.

You may find yourself communicating with your managers more often but do not forget the rest of the team. Everyone in the company needs some level of information about the downturn and how the turnaround will take place.

Team Meeting Outline

Regular weekly meetings are critical to present updates on the turnaround and field questions from the team. I realize this may seem like you are opening a can of worms, but it is far better than letting your staff come up with their own stories.

When it comes to having those tough conversations with your remaining team, such as big layoffs, here is an outline I have used for years.

1–Jump straight into the bad stuff and give the update. Don't sugar coat it. It's a need to know basis so you can leave out some details in your updates but get ahead of the negative issue and present it with honesty. It is okay to look nervous here, and in some cases, it is okay to show emotions. Be vulnerable and get it out there. Then let it sit for a moment before going to step 2.

2–Give a little good news about the bad news. There is always a way to spin the bad event into something better. Don't overdo it, and don't force it, but find something positive. Letting five employees go gives the other employees a chance to step up and prove themselves. Losing a significant client allows you to re-examine your retention strategies and find areas for improvement. Focus on how you and your employees can learn and grow from the experience.

3–The way forward. This step is critical, and it is what the employees will remember the most. What does the future look like? What are the next steps? Describe your plan, show the strategy, and give them something to believe in.

The staff will be looking to you for a level of confidence in the plan. Show your enthusiasm and faith in the turnaround plan, so they have something to believe in. You may need to push yourself here since your level of personal confidence in the plan may be tenuous but be the leader they need to see and sell it!

In addition to regular meetings, you may want to do a monthly email update to the entire team. Include high-level updates that help your staff see the progress. Often it is hard to see how much progress you have made until you recap what has been accomplished up to now. Any new employees can review old emails to get a sense of where the company has been and where it is heading.

Stronger Company Culture

At Survival Frog, our company culture improved after each hit we took. Layoffs and continued losses were tough to take, but we always kept the staff updated with our plan to move forward, and this helped us rally behind the efforts. We found ourselves communicating very openly with the remaining team, and everyone bonded together.

After layoffs, the productivity of our remaining employees skyrocketed. Everyone felt fortunate to still be at Survival Frog, and we all developed the collaborative attitude of working together to pull the turnaround off.

Chapter 28: Action Steps

➤ Come up with your talking points for team meetings. Commit to having team meetings once a week to keep everyone up-to-date on the company's progress.

CHAPTER 29
FINAL THOUGHTS ON LABOR EFFICIENCY

The most important thing in communication is to hear what isn't being said. ~Peter F. Drucker

Finding greater labor efficiency may be the most crucial aspect of your business turnaround. Taking action to reduce the employee count in your company, however, is one of the toughest parts of being an entrepreneur.

Forced Efficiency

Running an efficient company is an elusive goal for most business owners. When going through a downturn, however, it is something that will come quickly.

Efficiency is not a choice for a business suffering through a downturn; it is a requirement.

When you have a staff of 20 people and let half of them go, you are inflicting forced efficiency on the company. It is impossible to operate the way you did before. You must restructure departments to eliminate projects and get more work done in less time. Yes, it hurts, but it is the natural process of a turnaround and produces impressive results when completed.

I honestly don't think a company can become extremely efficient until faced with a major downturn. It sometimes takes heavy losses for the owner to realize just how much more efficient the company can become. Only when forced to let people go are you able to find ways to get more work done with fewer people (or at least get the right work done). That discipline forces you to run a lean, mean profit machine.

Parkinson's law states that "one's work expands to fill the time available for its completion," meaning that if an employee has eight hours to work, their tasks will increase to eight hours. Take away some of those hours, and you will find increased efficiency.

How exactly can your company become more efficient? How will you get more work done with fewer people and at a much lower cost? Every company is different, but I do know that you will find a way.

Your Company Will Not Look the Same

As I coach clients in the art of the turnaround, one of the most common struggles I see is business owners who do not want to rock the boat. Trying to keep your company the same as it was before, and avoiding big changes never works.

When you have completed a successful turnaround plan, your company will not look the same. Entrepreneurs fear that their beloved company will be changed for the worse or lose its way. That fear is real, but the truth is that if you survive your turnaround journey, your company's heart will only grow stronger.

Do not hang on to the old ways. They are the same ways that got you into this mess. Instead, welcome change and embrace a new way of operating your business. Create a company that produces profits well above industry standards. Your employees will be more engaged and your mission more focused. Good things will come from this if you are expecting them. But you need to expect change, and a lot of it.

Your #1 Job

Do not lose sight of your number one responsibility throughout this turnaround, which is to stay in business.

Keeping everyone happy, protecting employees, and maintaining past promises (both verbal and implied) takes a backseat to your top priority.

You must keep your business going, at all costs (but still legally and ethically). I have no doubt you will do right by people, but don't lose sight that you must put your business and your personal finances ahead of the emotions that come with finding your labor efficiency.

You did not ask for this, but it is here, and you must deal with it. It is necessary to take that one painful step backward to propel your company two or three steps forward.

Lean into it and take the action that you know is right. I promise, once it is all over, you will look back at these challenging times and be glad it happened. Although you cannot see it now, something good will come from this experience. It is here to make you and your company stronger.

Chapter 29: Action Steps

> ➤ Are you okay if your company looks drastically different but stays in business? Share your thoughts in your turnaround journal.

SECTION FIVE: FINDING LABOR EFFICIENCIES

SECTION SIX
THE TURNAROUND
PLAN

Don't wish for easy. Easy sucks, it invites competition and lower margins. Wish for the ability to overcome the inevitable challenges better than your competition. ~Byron

Here it is, the moment you have been waiting for - the section in this book where you finalize your own "Turnaround Plan".

Most struggling business owners are searching for that one big idea to act on to make all the problems go away and cause profit to come roaring back. They want something to clear up all the headaches, remove frustration and anxiety, and make the pain go away.

It is okay to want an easy and quick fix, and it's okay to keep looking for it, but the real solution to your dilemma will require many different moving parts.

A successful turnaround commonly demands that a company improve various operations and solve several problems at once. No two companies are ever the same, so your turnaround strategy will need to be original and specific.

SECTION SIX: THE TURNAROUND PLAN

In this book, you have already received dozens, if not hundreds, of suggestions and recommendations, a combination of which will comprise your turnaround plan. Take what you need to succeed, discard the rest, and build your company's specific and unique turnaround plan.

CHAPTER 30
TURNAROUND STRATEGIES

Sometimes when things are falling apart, they may actually be falling in place. ~Ron Douglas

This chapter will review some of the most common turnaround strategies. If you have not skipped right to this chapter looking for that magic bullet, none of this information will be new to you, because it has been covered in-depth earlier in the book. I will not repeat everything we previously explored and instead will identify the sections and chapters you can review for the comprehensive discussion.

Now is the time to connect the dots and see how everything works together.

Reduce Expenses–Fast! [Section 4]

It is ironic how most entrepreneurs prefer not to focus on cost-cutting, yet it is the single most impactful way to survive a downturn. Unlike the hit or miss strategy of increasing revenue, reducing expenses is something you control, and can be very predictable.

Remember the high leveraged $1:$1 ratio that cutting expenses has on the bottom line. Do not skip Section 4, which goes into detail on the various strategies for cutting expenses. Your goal should be to cut costs to match your new lower revenue levels. Lowering costs is the fastest, most effective way to turn your business around. Period.

Increase Revenue [Section 3]

"Finally…" you must be thinking, "this is the strategy I want to focus on." While I agree this should be an area of focus, you cannot rely on this strategy alone.

This strategy is listed here simply because it is the obvious one everyone expects to read about. However, increasing revenue is not predictable enough to base your turnaround on and this certainly cannot be your only strategy.

Optimize Existing Revenue [Section 3]

You may not even need to increase your revenue if you can work smarter with the income you already have coming in.

As explained in Chapter 16, you need to break down each revenue source into its own "rough" P&L to see the best and the worst revenue channels.

How can you optimize your best revenue sources by cutting operational costs or optimizing your marketing budget? How can you change the cost structure of your revenue, so that it is more profitable?

Then take a hard look at the dogs. In some cases, reducing or even completely removing poorly performing revenue channels can increase your company's profits. And you have the added benefit of simplifying the business and allowing you to focus on the better performing revenue sources.

Optimize Margins [Section 3]

Optimizing margins is a more in-depth look into your product or service. How can you increase your gross margin on your product line? Survival Frog went from 550 product SKUs to just 170. Only the highest margin products, with the highest volume of sales remained.

Then, Survival Frog raised prices on those remaining 170 products and substantially lowered the inbound shipping costs by reducing air freight. The result was a 50% increase in gross margin. How could you do something similar?

Service-based companies can achieve the same by finding ways to reduce labor costs. If you have ten features of your service, you could likely remove a few without your customer abandoning you. What features did your service have when you started your company? And how many did you add over the years? Consider getting back to basics and reducing your costs temporarily during your turnaround period. In Chapter 17 we explored strategies to increase the product or service margins so that every dollar you earn provides more contribution margin.

Simplify The Business [Sections 3, 4, 5]

When a company is growing, it can add new divisions, management levels and complicated projects. But when a company is in a downturn, it must be in a defensive position and streamline.

To turn around your business, you need to simplify your business. You will need to let go of some of your legacy projects and stop doing things "the way you've always done it." That can be difficult for entrepreneurs.

When simplifying your business, you may need to let some employees go. See Section 5 for help with this process. Layoffs mean you will need to get more done with fewer people.

Maybe you do not need to get more done. If you simplify your business, less needs to be done, allowing you to keep your expenses down.

Chapter 30: Action Steps

➢ From the five main turnaround approaches described in this chapter, which strategies apply most to your situation? You most likely will need to execute more than one strategy.

SECTION SIX: THE TURNAROUND PLAN

CHAPTER 31
THE PROFIT CORE
OF YOUR BUSINESS

Profit isn't a purpose, it's a result. To have purpose means the things we do are of real value to others.
~Simon Sinek

As with most things in life, there is a core where you can find the best of the best. Even in a failing business there is a core where things are still working well. Sometimes you must dig for it, but it is there - the profit core.

Your ability to find the profit core of your business could be the difference between a failed turnaround attempt and executing a powerful plan that gets you back to profitability.

Finding the core, then optimizing and growing it is key to your turnaround. The first profit core area to look at during a turnaround is the revenue the business is currently generating.

Revenue Channels:

As discussed in Section 3, the revenue channel contributing most to your profit core usually has the best margins and has the lowest cost. Often, it is the simplest revenue with the fewest problems. It may only be half or even one-third of the total revenue, but it is there.

Usually, the profit core is subsidizing other revenue channels that are losing money. When the losing revenue channels are removed, or minimized, the profit core can start to help the company realize its profit potential.

Your task is to break apart your revenue channels and determine your best and worst revenue sources. Then consider stripping away revenue channels that do *not* contribute to the profit core.

Products & Services:

If you have more than one product or service you offer customers, you will likely have a few that stand out from the rest as top performers.

Physical product companies often have hundreds or even thousands of different products that they sell. The 80/20 rule states 20% of the products (your core) generate 80% of the revenue. It is your job to determine which of the products are generating the best results (the profit core) and put more effort into this area.

If you are a services company, which of your services are the most profitable? How can you take what is working and do it even better? You may consider putting some services on hold if they are not producing enough profits – you can always bring them back later.

Employees:

Employees are a great example of the profit core, but instead of profit it is high value work you are looking for.

Take a piece of paper and list each of your employees and then rate them from the most valuable to the least. This is not your favorites list; this is actual value driven results that are producing profits.

The top half of the list is your profit core. The bottom half is where you can start reducing company size and expenses.

Marketing:

Paid marketing campaigns often have a core of what is working well, surrounded by a bunch of activity that is not working as well. This is not necessarily a bad thing during growth mode, but when losses start adding up it is time to take a second look at the marketing budget.

One common profit core area within marketing can be found with existing customer lists. Repeat buyers generate a lot more profit with lower costs so be sure you are allocating enough energy towards your best customers.

Projects:

Similar to marketing efforts, you will find that most of your company's projects and efforts can be put into 2 groups; those that are generating profits today and those that may produce profit in the future.

There never seems to an end of cool new projects, or as I call them "shiny objects" that you can be chasing. Some of these projects have real potential of improving the company in some way - in the future.

During moments of crisis you should not be focused so far into the future. Getting the company back to profitability must take priority over almost all future potential projects.

Challenges in Cutting Non-Core Activities

Even when it becomes obvious that cutting non-profit core activity is needed, it can prove to be difficult to take action. You may struggle with the decision to cut revenue, remove products, lay off employees or pause projects that are not feeding your profit core.

Shrinking the size of the business is agonizing and comes with all kinds of mental challenges. But when you focus in on your financials and build out P&L forecasts you can start to see the logic behind these changes.

Once you find your profit core and start to strip away everything else around it, you will find a healthy and profitable company. Although you may be left with a smaller company, you are still in business and can take pride in the fact that you are profitable once again.

Rebuilding From the Core Up

Don't worry, reducing the size of your company so that you can focus more on your core is not permanent. Once your turnaround plan starts working and you see profits again, you can start rebuilding.

Take that smaller version of your company and its core that is working so well and optimize it. Then scale it!

With high margins, you can do so much more in growing a company. Now that all the "bad revenue" and the distracting projects are out of your way, you can focus on building back to the level you were before.

This time, however, when you achieve the same revenue you had pre-downturn, you will be operating a high net margin business model that runs smoothly.

When you dial in your margins and have control over your expenses, you might be able to double or even triple your previous net profits. That's freakin' huge! You will be making more money, with less headache and less risk.

For example:

Pre downturn you may have found yourself with:

$10 million x 5% net margins = $500,000 net profit

Execute a turnaround and improve your net profits at a lower revenue level.

$3.3 million at 15% = $500,000 net profit

Then grow the company to previous levels but with higher margins:

$10 million at 15% = $1,500,000 net profit

Even if you do not grow back to pre-downturn revenue levels, you are *still* making more money. That is the power of finding the profit core of your business.

Chapter 31: Action Steps

> ➤ Define your profit core for each area: revenue channels, products and services, employees, marketing, and projects. Focus more on your profit core and start trimming away everything else.

CHAPTER 32
WHEN TO CALL IT QUITS

*Take it behind the barn and shoot it. ~Kevin
O'Leary, Shark Tank*

You are flying a broken airplane. It has numerous
mechanical issues. You are dangerously low on fuel, and
the runway is too far away.

You are about to crash the plane. However, you do not
need to hit the side of the mountain and go up in a ball of
flame. There may be a way to land somewhere and salvage
parts of the plane.

In this chapter, we will discuss how you can crash land your
plane (business) and salvage parts of your credit and

personal wealth. First, let's talk about how to know if your company is doomed to crash.

Four ways to know it is time to call it quits:

#1–Listen To the Math

Logically speaking, your business's survival will come down to the math. You can still possess the desire to save your company but if the numbers are not working, you will need to be honest with yourself and take a hard look at the facts. There are two areas where the math can spell trouble.

The first is cash to operate your business. If you run out of money in the bank, you will either need to contribute additional capital or shut the company down.

That is why we focus so much on cashflow and knowing your cash runway. Putting more cash into your business makes sense in some situations but be careful since it can be a slippery slope. At some point, it is just throwing good money after bad.

The second area you can predict your demise is with your forecasted P&L statements. I am not talking about your current P&L's. Those are most likely showing heavy losses, but those losses will turn if you have the right turnaround plan.

It is the forecasted P&L's that you need to examine. If you cannot get a future P&L to show a profit before running out of cash, then the business is screaming at you to shut it down.

Assuming your forecasts are realistic, conservative, and show a potential profit down the road, there is still hope.

Survival Frog lost money for over 12 months, but we knew if we could reduce our expenses to meet the new revenue levels, we had a fighting chance to survive.

If you cannot get a forecasted P&L to show profit eventually, it will be less about your desire to succeed and more about the math.

#2–Feedback Loop

As you develop your turnaround plan, you should be seeking advice and feedback from business associates and friends who are running successful businesses. If the feedback you are receiving is that perhaps you should shut things down, you need to consider the advice you are receiving.

However, if one or two people hint that you should shut down your business, it does not necessarily mean you should. Take their recommendations and process them, but make your decision based on all your information.

I had three people (out of about 40) tell me, in so many words, that I should shut down my business. I did not. I turned Survival Frog around in the end. So, it is not like you must act on the advice you are getting.

You are the filter of all information relating to your downturn – take input from people, compare it with your other findings, and make your own decisions.

Another consideration of feedback is when people are not completely honest with you. Your friends and associates respect you and want to be kind. That is great until they start telling you what you want to hear. "I have confidence in you, keep fighting," can be encouraging to hear, but not if it is merely prolonging the inevitable.

If you sincerely want their advice, spin the question around and ask them head-on: "I am thinking about shutting the company down. What are your thoughts?" You can ask that question even if you are not ready to shut down, but this type of question will allow them to be more honest.

As mentioned earlier in the book, your job is to collect all the feedback you can from different people. Then, filter the information, find trends, connect the dots, and come up with your own conclusions.

The reason that getting feedback from other people is so important is they are not as close to the problem as you are. You are likely so close that you cannot see the problem for what it really is. Getting an unbiased view from one of your business friends can be a great way to see the big picture and come up with new solutions.

#3–You Have Lost Your Drive

If you have lost your drive and motivation to run your company, it may be time to call it quits.

Of course, during a downturn, you most likely have that sentiment at some point almost every week. It is important you consider your emotions in the context of what is going on. You are allowed to have bad days, and bad weeks, but if you find yourself in a *constant* state of despair about the business, you should take a closer look at your drive for running the business.

During my downturn, I had many over-anxious days, where I was 100% sure I wanted to quit, and almost pulled the trigger to shut down the business. By the next day, it turned into a 90% feeling, then 80%, and over time the feelings would subside.

So, when you have these feelings, give it a day. You will most likely feel better tomorrow or next week. However, if the feeling never subsides, you may have a more significant issue on your hands.

If you felt burned out with the business before the downturn, this could be another meaningful sign that you have lost your drive.

#4–Market Outlook

Has something changed in the market that makes it impossible to move your business forward? For example, suppose you owned a restaurant and were barely hitting profitability with full capacity. Now, COVID-19 restrictions force you to reduce to 50% capacity for the foreseeable future. Do the math.

Look at the facts of the market. Maybe your primary supplier is discontinuing production. There could be new, cost-prohibitive government regulations you must follow.

Sometimes, the facts of the market make it logistically impossible to continue to run your business.

Markets and business categories go through cycles. They go down, then go back up. If it is going to be a few years before the next swing up, you may see this as a chance to downsize and wait for the market to come back. There will be less competition, and this could work out well for you. Or maybe it will be five or ten years before things return to normal, if ever. You need to consider the timeline and how long you are willing to wait.

For some businesses, it is a struggle to stay afloat even in good times. If your business model is flawed, a downturn will expose the model for what it is.

Consider Your Exit Plan in Advance

You may believe an exit plan only applies to those who are selling a business, but you can use this similar thought process to shut things down properly.

You can and should formulate your exit plan now, even if you are still holding out hope for a successful turnaround. The act of thinking through how you can shut things down will allow your mind to stop worrying as much. If you have a rough plan, then you can let go of the worrying of what it would look like – and get back to saving your business.

The process of thinking through how to shut down my business helped me calm my anxiety levels. I had a rough plan so if things ever did get to the point of shutting down, I had already thought through the critical elements of exiting the business. I pre-planned such things as which bankruptcy attorney I would use, what payments I should stop paying first, how I would close the company and how I would move forward and earn money to support my family.

This "Plan F" was how I could shut down the company and protect as much of my wealth and credit rating as possible.

Protect Your Personal Assets and Credit

Let's get back to flying your broken airplane. Like it or not, you are the pilot, and everyone on board is looking to you to save the day:

Engine #1 is gone.

Engine #2 is smoking.

Your landing gear is stuck. You are dangerously low on fuel.

It is a full-blown Defcon 5 emergency.

The plane is going down; at this point, it is inevitable. However, your job is to keep it from crashing into the side of a cliff and taking everyone on board with it.

Your objective is to crash land this thing and get it on the ground in one piece. Then maybe you can sell the scrap metal.

As if going through a downturn was not agonizing enough, now you are tasked with shutting things down. You may even be tempted to push the yoke down and just go out in a ball of flame. This is not the best approach.

There is more than the business at stake. You may be facing potential lawsuits or foreclosures that could affect your personal assets. Small business owners often have personal guarantees in place with their businesses, so even your personal credit is at risk here.

There may be options for strategic reorganization and bankruptcy that can protect your assets. These legal strategies are far beyond this book's scope, but I recommend you find a trustworthy attorney to help you through the process.

Just like you put your turnaround plan in writing, you need to put your exit plan in writing. What steps can you take to crash land the plane while protecting your credit and your personal assets? Are there company assets you can sell off to pay or settle part of your debt?

Even if you are still fighting to keep the airplane in the air, planning a potential exit plan makes sense. Going through the "what if..." activity during your turnaround can give you a little peace of mind. If things ever get so bad that you cannot save the company, you already have a plan. This should allow you stop worrying about the worst-case scenario and go back to running your company.

It Does Not Have to Be All or Nothing

Instead of shutting everything down, can you just "pause" the business? Or can you take it down to just one or two people and run it in maintenance mode until the market returns?

Maybe there is a way to scale the business down to its bare bones and still take a modest salary to live off until you find your next business move.

If you can maintain one of your revenue sources with minimal effort, this could be an alternative to shutting everything down. For Survival Frog, my "Plan F" was to shut everything down, sell all the inventory, and just operate our email list. I would be able to send affiliate offers to the email list and generate enough money to support my family.

Do you have service contracts you can maintain and earn a living from? Do you have accounts receivable that can provide cashflow to live off for six months as you regroup?

There are many variations of shutting down that do not involve crashing your airplane into the cliff's side, so give it thought and come up with your own plan F.

Regroup and Move On

Personally, I have seen my share of failures in business. With each stumble, I can look back now with gratitude that everything worked out exactly the way it did.

With each business failure you learn what works and what to avoid in the future. Adversity is the best teacher and is an essential part of becoming a better businessperson.

Thomas Edison said *"I have not failed. I've just found 10,000 ways that won't work."*

Without the failures I experienced behind me; I would have never found the next company in my entrepreneur journey. If it was not for the previous businesses shutting down, I might still be working in a dead-end business that didn't have potential–those failures led me to bigger and better things.

It does not feel like it at the time, but often the challenges you are currently facing could be the best thing for you. I am not sure where you are at with your business but consider that maybe all this is a good thing.

Chapter 32: Action Steps

> ➢ If it ever comes down to it, what is your exit plan? How would you shut down the business while protecting your credit and personal assets? It is better to have a rough plan and not ever need it than to stress over what the future may hold.

CHAPTER 33
THE BEST $85 OF MY LIFE

Failure should be our teacher, not our undertaker.
Failure is a delay, not defeat. It is a temporary detour,
not a dead end. ~Denis Waitley

This section is all about you and your turnaround. You have received hundreds of suggestions to use in your own turnaround plan, and while I have shared many ways that we came up with Survival Frog's turnaround, I have tried to keep the focus on you and your company.

Our success in turning Survival Frog around is what prompted me to share my experiences, and so it is fitting to share with you that pivotal moment when we knew the tides were turning.

SECTION SIX: THE TURNAROUND PLAN

One of the most exciting moments of our turnaround was the month when we accurately forecasted and proceeded to lose $20,000.

It was not the $20,000 loss that was exciting, but rather our ability to forecast the loss. The forecast numbers had stopped bouncing around wildly, and we were able to predict the future P&L. What was even more exciting was that we were showing a profit coming up in two months.

The following month, we lost money again, but it matched our forecast. Exciting losses, right? The next month was going to be profitable, and we had confidence in our projections. Sure enough, the third month rolled along, and we were profitable. We made $85 net profit.

The best $85 of my life!

We did it! We were operating in the black! Then it got extremely exciting because as we projected out the next few months, we saw higher and higher profits each month. Eventually we started seeing net profits margins that were three times our pre downturn levels.

Survival Frog remained very profitable over the next ten months. The business was running more smoothly than ever and required less of my time. Most of my competitors had closed up their businesses due to the market downturn and Survival Frog gained a lot of market share. Then in early 2020 COVID-19 happened, and that changed everything.

As you might expect, the Coronavirus pandemic and the unrest that followed created a massive demand for survival products. The market was back, and Survival Frog was healthy and growing again.

We quickly regained the revenue drop we experienced during the downturn and found ourselves back at pre-downturn revenue levels. But now things were different. Now the business ran ultra-efficiently and we could handle the rapid growth with far fewer challenges.

There were growing pains and we rapidly hired new team members and expanded the company. However, we only required a fraction of the team we once had. What took us 27 employees a few years ago, now needed just 9 people to operate. We were at the same revenue but with 1/3 of the employees required to run the company, which helped us maintain strong net profit margins.

So how did we go from massive losses to industry-leading profit margins? **We analyzed our situation, created a turnaround plan, and executed it.**

Additional revenue is not what saved us, although we fought like hell to increase it during the downturn. What rescued us was the turnaround plan that we put into place. It was executing a combination of the strategies and tactics summarized below.

Survival Frog's Turnaround Strategy Can Work For You Too

Five primary turnaround strategies were used in Survival Frog's recovery. Each has been described in detail throughout the pages of this book. Let's recap so that you can decide if any of the strategies apply to your business.

1–Restructure & simplify

You may need to change the company to become more efficient and often this means getting smaller. For Survival Frog it was eliminating our IT department and automating our accounting department. We closed our office and warehouse, worked virtually, and hired an outside company to handle the order fulfillment.

Are there departments in your company where you could simplify or even restructure? Which projects can you eliminate or put on hold for 6 months? Create your own "stop doing" list and streamline your business so you are focusing only on profit core areas.

2–Optimize revenue

Removing poor performing revenue will help you get back on level ground. We eliminated $1 million of "bad" revenue and were able to spend more time and energy optimizing our profitable revenue.

Divide up your revenue channels and examine the data. Optimize the winners and cut the losers.

3—Improve gross margins

Both service-related businesses and physical product companies can work on improving gross margins. Survival Frog cut 550 products down to the 170 with the best margins, highest volume, and easiest fulfillment. Then, we went to work optimizing our margins on those high-performing products by lowering manufacturing costs, raising prices and restructuring shipping costs. The end results were an increase to our gross margin by 50%.

How can your prices and cost structure be optimized to improve your gross margins? Examine the top 20% of your products or services – how can you spend more of your focus in this area?

4—Reduce expenses

Finally, we reduced our expenses deeper and further than we ever thought possible over several waves of cutbacks.

What are the immediate cost cuts you know you need to make? Complete your color-coded spreadsheet and get control over your expenses.

5—Master the art of financial analysis

The answer is always found within the financials, so this is not an area you can ignore or delegate to your accounting manager. For me personally, it was the most valuable skill I have learned, and I am grateful for the downturn giving me this new skillset.

You must step up to the plate and become a master of your financial reports. You will be glad you did. Get your cashflow forecast set up, then start to analyze your P&L's so you can start to forecast your financial future.

Chapter33: Action Steps

> What will your turnaround success story look like? Document in your turnaround journal how you will feel, who you will thank later, and what life will be like moving forward.

CONCLUSION

Success is a false teacher. Failures teach you far more and prepare you for your next big success. ~Byron

The Struggle Is the Way

Every successful entrepreneur has failed their way to success. Failure is not a character flaw, but merely a temporary circumstance, a momentary result from a combination of factors.

Having a business on the brink of disaster takes a toll on you personally. The stress, mental anguish, and financial uncertainty are all emotions that can drain your spirit and energy.

313

Never underestimate how much an entrepreneur's life is tied to his or her business. Interwoven into your business are your personal finances, your pride, and your spirit. Your livelihood is on the line, and possibly your personal assets. When your business is hurting, so are you.

Everyone is holding their breath, waiting to see if you will recover. Your family, employees, and perhaps even your customers are looking to you for solutions. There is enormous pressure to fix the problem and to fix it now.

Yet through this turnaround journey you will grow. You will find the strength within to push through adversity and to become a better person for it.

The seed of adversity can blossom into an abundance of opportunity. Struggle breeds wisdom. Wisdom helps you find a better way forward despite your past mistakes.

The Turnaround Gift

While your challenges can feel overwhelming, the rewards can be monumental. Adversity is a strange gift, but it *is* a gift. With the challenges, you grow and become stronger. Your business will be healthier, more efficient, and much more profitable.

If you have moments of doubt, welcome to the club. Keep fighting even if you do not know if you will endure. Failure is often just a state of mind, and you may not see the light at the end of the tunnel until the very end of the ordeal.

Given a little time and distance after you complete your turnaround, things *will* start to look different. I predict that when this is all over, you will have a new-found respect for your ability to overcome the challenges in your life.

Many people who have gone through a downturn (including me), come away from it thinking that the downturn was the best thing that could have happened. In fact, you may not be able to imagine ever going back to how things used to be!

However, amid your downturn (or any challenge in your life), it is impossible to see beyond your current despair. You simply cannot see the bright side of life when you are caught up in an EF-5 tornado. There is too much debris flying and fear surging through your body. All you can do is have faith.

Have faith that when it is all over, you will look back and appreciate the ordeal. **Something good will come from this.** What is happening now is happening for a reason, and you will eventually be grateful for the experience.

This does not mean you should just sit back and surrender to the downturn. You need to stand your ground and fight every step of the way.

Maybe, the Universe is preparing you. Could this downturn be the catalyst that pushes you in the right direction and leads you to a much better business in the future? If you are looking for the good in the experience, you are likely to find it.

Imagine you hired a high-level CFO to help your business. Would you prefer to hire a CFO that has only had success in his or her past? Or would you instead hire the guy that has taken companies that were knee-deep in a downturn, full of major issues, and turned the company around? I am sure you would agree that the second CFO, who has been through hell and back, is significantly more valuable than the one who has only seen good times. Those battle scars are worth a lot and will make you more valuable to your business, or your next undertaking. It really is a gift.

Your Turnaround Plan

Every turnaround plan is different. Your company cannot use Survival Frog's exact step-by-step sequence, just like the business down the street could not duplicate your turnaround plan. Use the advice and guidance in this book in drafting your own turnaround plan.

Here is your action plan:

1–Increase cashflow runway. First things first, increase your cash runway, and monitor it closely with your cashflow forecast sheet. Cash in the bank buys you time to fix the business.

2–Analyze P&L historical and forecasting. Use percentages to show changes between the good times and current challenges. What has changed to cause your losses?

What must you do to fix it going forward? Build a P&L forecast to see how those changes will affect your company.

3–Create a rough turnaround plan. Put it in writing and lay out your initial turnaround plans. Make big, bold moves and rally your team.

4–Finetune your turnaround plan. Once the above changes are in motion, take more time to analyze the data. Fine tune your cashflow forecast and P&L forecasting. Get feedback from other entrepreneurs and financial experts. Find your profit core–then make another round of big, bold changes.

5–Optimize and simplify the business. It is more than just cutting costs; you must also find efficiencies and optimize the profit core of the company.

The turnaround plan provides steps and processes to work through each intricate part of the downturn, one move at a time. It allows you to see into the future with P&L forecasts and provides confidence that your ideas will work.

Final Words

As I write these final words in The *Small Business Turnaround Plan*, it is late-2020, and the world is finding its way through the COVID-19 crisis. Small businesses in the United States struggle to find new footing and deal with the uncertain times in which we live. The economic and social changes create a need for thousands of small businesses to develop a turnaround plan.

While some businesses are taking a wait and see approach, other entrepreneurs have responded boldly to the situation and are making courageous changes. Now is the time to design your own "change" environment for your company. Instead of hoping for another government stimulus package or waiting for things to get "back to normal," you can create change by embracing new ideas and streamlining your business.

Meet the market where it is today. Get your cost structure down to your current revenue levels and then wait for the market to return. Be profitable while you wait out the storm. It is acceptable to be smaller; it is okay to be different from the next guy. This, too, shall pass, and you will be in a better position to build back up once the storm has passed.

The single most significant contributor to a business's chance for success is *the speed at which it moves*.

When the owner or CEO moves too slowly and does not make tough decisions fast enough, the company is at considerable risk. The clock is ticking, and every week you delay making bold decisions is that much less cash you will have in your bank to survive.

You must act quickly and decisively. Do not worry about perfection; you will be making lots of changes along the way. Just get started, and the rest will fall into place.

Business downturns come with a lot of fear and uncertainty. I challenge you to use that fear to your advantage.

Which definition of "fear" will you choose?

F-E-A-R – Forget Everything And Run

or

F-E-A-R – Face Everything And Rise

The choice is yours.

There is tremendous satisfaction that comes with executing a turnaround plan. Once you get to the flip side, you will feel more satisfied in your business and personal life. You will be a role model to others as someone who overcame the odds.

In the introduction of this book, I asked you to do just one thing, if you recall. I asked that you "allow your mind to move beyond impossible." Believe there is always a way to push forward with your ideas.

You might not know from the start what your final solution will be, or what your company will look like in the end but begin the process. You will gain confidence along the way, and clarity comes with time.

The next step is yours and yours alone. Take it, and you will be one step closer to building the leaner, more profitable, and stable company you have always wanted. Believe your company can overcome the impossible and that you will achieve success with your turnaround plan.

OTHER RESOURCES

Thank you so much for your purchase of this book and your time investment to work through the Small Business Turnaround Plan.

OTHER RESOURCES:

- Entrepreneurs Organization (EO), has local chapters in most major cities around the world. If you are looking for ways to create meaningful connections with other small business owners this is where you want to be. www.EOnetwork.org
- If your company needs an "operating system" to become more systematic and organized, then I recommend *Traction* by Wickman or *Scaling Up* by Harnish. We use EOS from Traction to effectively run Survival Frog. This changed everything for us.

ABOUT THE AUTHOR

Byron Walker has been a serial entrepreneur for the last 20 years. He currently owns and operates SurvivalFrog.com, one of the largest and most well-known e-commerce store in the survival niche.

Byron is known as a direct response marketing expert and specializes in sales funnel optimization and scaling direct to consumer businesses. He is an active board member of Entrepreneurs' Organization (EO).

Living in Denver, Colorado, Byron and his family enjoy skiing, water sports, camping and spending time outdoors.

To connect with Byron, reach out via LinkedIn (just be sure to mention something about the book): linkedin.com/in/walkerbyron.

ABOUT SNOWY RIDGE BOOKS

Being published and self-published book authors ourselves, we have experienced the same peaks and troughs of emotions and challenges as most authors.

We have developed a new way to develop non-fiction book content that completely removes the negative experiences associated with traditional writing.

While our books are published under the Snowy Ridge Books label, we provide training and support for our content development method through our sister website: ProduceMyBook.com

Produce My Book provides you with many benefits beyond traditional book publishing:

- Create your initial manuscript faster, usually within two weeks.
- Eliminate writer's block and enjoy producing content again!
- Reduce frustration by not having to type your manuscript from a blank page.
- Save money by not having to hire a writing coach or ghost writer.
- Increase content quality by producing more complete content than you would generate on your own.
- Get e-book AND printed books without having to pay up-front printing costs.

- Enjoy the process because you are working closely, one-on-one, with our staff from beginning to launch.

Go to ProduceMyBook.com to watch our free signature talk describing our non-fiction book development process in detail.

If you would not normally take the time to write a book, or have tried to write a book for years, here is your chance to share your expert method with the world!

Snowy Ridge Books
PO Box 441024
Aurora, CO 80044-1024
ProduceMyBook.com
crew@ProduceMyBook.com